Walter Raleigh, Alexander B. Grosart

Choice Passages from the Writings and Letters of Sir Walter Raleigh

Walter Raleigh, Alexander B. Grosart

Choice Passages from the Writings and Letters of Sir Walter Raleigh

ISBN/EAN: 9783337135058

Printed in Europe, USA, Canada, Australia, Japan

Cover: Foto ©ninafisch / pixelio.de

More available books at **www.hansebooks.com**

Choice Paſſages from the Writings and Letters of Sir Walter Raleigh;

being a ſmall Sheaf of Gleanings from a golden Harveſt by Alexander B. Groſart

LONDON
ELLIOT STOCK, 62, Paternoster Row
1893

INTRODUCTION.

The present booklet does not give a tithe of the copy prepared for the press after all manner of reluctant reduction and sifting. Sooth to say, half a score of volumes of identical quality should still leave many

'brave translunary things'

to be sought out by the 'gentle reader' (to return on the old kindly phrase). Was it Sheridan who said of the notorious Dr. Dodd's 'Beauties of Shakespeare,' 'Yes; very good—but where are the rest?' I fear the same retort may be made upon me, and, indeed, in relation to the entire series of which this forms one. But be it remembered extenuatingly, that one 'motif' in the preparation of this 𝔈lizabethan 𝔏ibrary is to stimulate, not to exhaust, interest in the supreme literature of those 'spacious days.' That 'motif' will be defeated unless in each successive case our relatively slight readings send our readers to the complete works.

Our CHOICE PASSAGES *from Raleigh (or*

as he mainly spelled his name, Ralegh;
albeit I have seen both at Hatfield and
Lismore Castle, and elsewhere, ' Raleigh')
are meant to serve a double end, viz., to
present him as Writer and as Man. That
is to say, an endeavour has been made to
bring together representative quotations
whereby to illustrate his distinction of style,
the stately march of his sentences, his cul-
tured allusiveness, his picked and packed
words, and at the same time to preserve
personal traits of character, opinion, and
sentiment, and the lights and shadows of
his many-sided and splendid career—the
career of an Englishman of high heroic
mould, whose simple name abides a spell
to all the English-speaking race. I confess
that a lump comes to my throat as I read
his ' Farewell Letters' (pp. 30-40) and
' Defences' (pp. 71-102). That such a
head should have been struck off is of the
infamies of our island-story. One inevitably
pronounces it damnable, that it should have
been possible for four sovereigns of England
in succession to perpetrate judicial murders
of this type and the nation be dumb—
Henry VIII., of More; Elizabeth, of
Essex; James I., of Raleigh; and
Charles I., of Strafford and Eliot.

Introduction.

It is remarkable how the least and most private letters, as the most self-evidently communicated learning, takes a stamp of noticeableness, either of thought, or turn of wording, or of graciousness.

I have resisted the temptation of annotating a number of places that invitingly lend themselves thereto, e.g., the stinging 'epitaphs' on Salisbury and Leicester—the former immortally gibbeted by Spenser in 'Mother Hubberd's Tale,' his terrible letter about Essex, his 'Instructions' to his son—given happily in completeness—his 'Defences' of his Guiana enterprise, his prison-books (p. 162), and the like. It had been a superfluous show of cheap learning to have marred the symmetry of the page by insertion of minute tracings of trite classical quotations and references.

This is hardly the place or occasion to intermeddle with the elder D'Israeli's literary (or unliterary) 'mare's nest' of the (so-called) 'secret history' of the History of the World—seeing that he is constrained to admit that for 'magnificence of eloquence and massiveness of thought we must still dwell on his pages,' and that undoubtedly 'all the eloquent, the grand, and the pathetic passages interspersed in the venerable volume,' were his own ('Curiosities of Literature,' iii., pp. 113, 132).

The following are the fuller titles of the several books from which these CHOICE PASSAGES have been gleaned, with our signs:

a. The History of the World (ed. 1614, folio) = H. W.
b. Maxims of State = M.
c. The Cabinet-Council, containing the chief arts of Empire and Mysteries of State (originally published by Milton) = Cab.
d. The Discoverie of Guiana = 'Discoverie.'
e. The Prerogative of Parliaments = P. of P.
f. Instructions to his Son and Posterity—complete.
g. Letters (from Edwards' 'Life and Letters') = Letters.
h. Poems.

The last ('Poems') are, alas! limited to two — the subtle and cunningly-wrought love-poems, the second of which drew from Alp. Trench an unusually fervent tribute of praise ('Household Book of English Poetry'), and the great LAST LINES.

Introduction.

The only presently-available collective edition of the Works of Raleigh is the utterly unworthy one from 'the University Press' of Oxford (8 vols., 1829). For his complete Poems see Archdeacon Hannay's admirable Aldine edition—a charming book.

A. B. G.

St. George's Vestry,
    Blackburn, Lancashire.

CONTENTS.

	PAGE
Adonijah and Barsheba	1
Ambition and Glory	2
Biography	2
Church	3
Chronology	7
Conscience	8
Consolation	9
Controversy	12
Duelling and Pseudo-Honour	14
Eastern Position	23
Epitaphs	24
Elizabeth	25
Equivocation	26
Earl of Essex	27
Fame	29
Farewell Letters	30
Fate and Free Will and Astrology	41
Geography	47
Great Men	49
God—Creation and Providence	50
Guiana and its Colonisation	71

Contents.

	PAGE
Honour	102
Injustice	103
Instinct	105
Kings and Kingdoms, including 'Brave and Noble Words to James I.'	107
Rules and Axioms for preserving of A KINGDOM hereditary or conquered	122
Law	130
Life and Death	133
Moral Government of the Universe	147
Treason—Injustice of Arraignment	158
Prison-Books	163
Posterity, Instructions to his Son and	165
My own Times	191
History—its Rights and Dignity	193
English v. Roman and French Valour	195
To his Mistress, Queen Elizabeth	198
A Poesy to prove Affection is not Love	200
Verses found in his Bible in the Gatehouse at Westminster, 1618	202

ADONIJAH AND BARSHEBA.

In ... his weak estate of body, when David was in a manner bedrid, Adonijah, his eldest son (Amnon and Absalom being now dead) having drawn unto his party that invincible, renowned, and feared Joab, with Abiathar the priest, began manifestly to prepare for his establishment in the kingdom after his father. For being the eldest now living of David's sons, and a man of goodly personage—Solomon yet young, and born of a mother formerly attainted with adultery: for which her name was omitted by St. Matthew, (as Bede, Hugo, [St.] Thomas [Aquinas], and others suppose) he presumed to carry the matter without resistance. (H. W., B. ii., c. xvii.)

AMBITION AND GLORY.

If we seek a reason of the succession and continuance of this boundless ambition in mortal men, we may add.... that the kings and princes of the world have always laid before them the actions but not the ends of those great ones which preceded them. They are always transported with the glory of the one, but they never mind the misery of the other till they find the experience in themselves. They neglect the advice of God, while they enjoy life, or hope; but they follow the counsel of Death upon his first approach. (H. W., B. v., c. vi.)

TRIFLES IN BIOGRAPHY.

I think it not impertinent sometimes to relate such accidents as may seem no better than mere trifles; for even by trifles are the qualities of great persons as well disclosed as by their great actions; because in matters of importance they commonly strain themselves to the observance of general commended rules; in lesser things they follow the current of their own natures. (H. W., B. iv., c. v.)

THE CHURCH.
Laban not ' out of the Church.'

Although it be the opinion of St. Chrysostom and some later writers, as Cajetan, Oleaster, Musculus, Calvin, Mercer, and others, that Laban was an idolater because he retained certain idols or household gods which Rachel stole from him; yet that he believed in the true God, it cannot be denied. For he acknowledgeth the God of Abraham and of Nahor, and he called Abraham's servant blessed of Jehovah, as aforesaid. So, as for myself, I dare not avow that these men were out of the Church, who, sure I am, were not out of the faith. (H. W., B. ii., c. i.)

The Tabernacle—reverence for the Church.

This was the order of the army of Israel and of their encamping and marching: the Tabernacle of God being always set in the middle and centre thereof. The reverent care which Moses, the prophet and chosen servant of God, had in all that belonged even to the outward and least parts of the Tabernacle, Ark, and Sanctuary, witnessed well the inward and most humble zeal borne towards God Himself. The industry used in the framing thereof, and every and the least part thereof; the curious workmanship thereon bestowed; the exceeding charge and expense of the provisions; the dutiful observance in the laying up and preserving the holy vessels; the solemn renewing thereof; the vigilant attendance thereon, and the prudent defence of the same, which all ages have in some degree imitated, is now so forgotten and cast away in this superfine age, by those of THE FAMILY, by the Anabaptist, the Brownist, and other sectaries, as all cost and care bestowed and had of the Church wherein God is to be revered and worshipped is accounted a kind of Popery, and as proceeding from an idolatrous disposition; insomuch as time would soon bring to pass (if it were not resisted) that God would be turned out of churches into barns, and from thence again into the fields and mountains and under the hedges; and the offices of the ministry (robbed of all dignity and respect) be as contemptible as those places; all order, discipline, and church government left to newness of opinion and men's fancy; yea, and soon after as many kinds of religions spring up as there are parish churches within England; every contentious and ignorant person clothing his fancy with the "Spirit of God," and his imagination with "the gift of revelation"; insomuch as when the truth which is lost, and shall appear to the simple multitude no less variable than contrary to itself, the faith of men will soon after die away by degrees, and all religion be held in scorn and contempt. (H. W., B. ii., c. v.)

DAGON AND THE ARK OF GOD.

The Philistines returning with the greatest victory and glory which ever they obtained, carried the Ark of God with them to Azotus, and set it up in the house of Dagon, their idol; but that night the idol fell out of his place from above to the ground, and lay under the Ark. The morning following they took it up and set it again in his place, and it fell the second time, and the head brake from the body, and the hands from the arms, showing that it had nor power nor understanding in the presence of God; for the head fell off, which is the seat of reason and knowledge, and the hands (by which we execute strength) were sundered from the arms. For God and the Devil inhabit not in one house, nor in one heart. And if this idol could not endure the representative of the true God, it is not to be marvelled that at such time as it pleased Him to cover His only-begotten with flesh and sent Him into the world, that all the oracles wherein the Devil derided and betrayed mortal men lost power, speech and operation at the instant. For when that true Light which had never beginning of brightness, brake through the clouds of a virgin's body, shining upon the earth which had been long obscured by idolatry, all those foul and stinking vapours vanifhed. Plutarch rehearfeth a memorable accident in that age concerning the death of the great god Pan, as he ftyleth him; where (as ignorant of the true caufe), he fearcheth his brains for many reafons of fo great an alteration; yet finds he none out but frivolous. For not only this old devil did then die, as he fuppofed, but all the reft, as Apollo, Jupiter, Diana, and the whole rabble became fpeechlefs. (H. W., B. ii., c. xv.)

CHRONOLOGY.

SINCE I do here enter into that never refolved queftion and labyrinth of times [=Chronology], it behoveth me to give reafon for my own opinion; and with fo much the greater care and circumfpection, becaufe I walk afide and in a way apart from the multitude; yet not alone and without companions, though the fewer in numbers; with whom I rather choofe to endure the wounds of thofe darts which Envy cafteth at Novelty, than to go fafely and fleepily in the easy ways of ancient mistakings; seeing to be learned in many errors, as to be ignorant in all things, hath little diversity. (H. W., B. ii., c. i.)

CONSCIENCE.

A Clear Conscience.

For myself, if I have in anything served my Country, and prized it before my private; the general acceptation can yield me no other profit at this time, than doth a fair sunshine day to a seaman after shipwreck; and the contrary, no other harm than an outrageous tempest after the port attained. I know that I lost the love of many for my fidelity towards her [Queen Elizabeth] whom I must still honour in the dust; though further than the defence of her excellent person, I never persecuted [= opposed] any man. Of those that did it, and by what device they did it, He that is the supreme Judge of all the world hath taken the account. So as for this kind of suffering, I must say with Seneca, *Mala opinio, bene parta, delectat.*

Sir Walter Raleigh.

So for other men; if there be any that have made themselves fathers of that fame which hath been begotten for them, I can neither envy at such their purchased glory, nor much lament mine own mishap in that kind; but content myself to say with Virgil, *Sic vos non vobis*, in many particulars. (Preface, H. W.)

CONSOLATION.—ON DEATH OF LADY CECIL, 1596-7.
To Sir Robert Cecil.

SIR,—Because I know not how you dispose of yourself, I forbear to visit you; preferring your pleasing before mine own desire. I had rather be with you now than at any other time if I could thereby either take off from you the burden of your sorrows, or lay the greater part thereof on mine own heart. In the meantime I would but mind you of this, that you should not overshadow your wisdom with passion, but look aright into things as they are.

There is no man sorry for death itself, but only for the time of death; everyone knowing that it is a bond never forfeited to God. If, then, we know the same to be certain and inevitable, we ought withal to take the time of his arrival in as good part as the knowledge, and not to lament at the inſtant of every ſeeming adverſity, which, we are aſſured, have been on their way towards us from the beginning. It appertaineth to every man of a wiſe and worthy ſpirit to draw together into ſufferance the unknown future to the known preſent; looking no leſs with the eyes of the mind than thoſe of the body—the one beholding afar off and the other at hand—that thoſe things of this world in which we live be not ſtrange unto us when they approach, as to feebleneſs which is moved with novelties. But that like true men, participating immortality and knowing our deſtinies to be of God, we do then make our eſtates and works, our fortunes and deſires, all one.

It is true that you have loſt a good and virtuous wife, and myſelf an honourable friend and kinſwoman. But there was a time when ſhe was unknown to you, for whom you then lamented not. She is now no more, no more yours, nor of your acquaintance; but immortal, and not needing or knowing your love or sorrow. Therefore you shall but grieve for that which now is as then it was, when not yours; only bettered by the difference in this, that she hath past the wearisome journey of this dark world, and hath possession of her inheritance. She hath left behind her the fruit of her love; for whose sakes you ought to care for yourself, that you leave them not without a guide, and not by grieving to repine at His will that gave them you, or by sorrowing to dry up your own times that ought to establish them.

I believe it that sorrows are dangerous companions, converting bad into evil and evil into worse, and do no other service than multiply harm. They are the treasures of weak hearts and of the foolish. The mind that entertaineth them is as the earth and dust, whereon sorrows and adversities of the world do, as the beasts of the field, tread, trample and defile. The mind of man is that part of God which is in us, which, by how much it is subject to passion, by so much it is further from Him that gave it us. Sorrows draw not the dead to life, but the living to death. And if I were myself to advise myself in the like, I would never forget my patience till I saw all and the worst of evils, and so grieve for all at once; lest lamenting for some one another might not remain in the power of Destiny of greater discomfort.

Yours ever beyond the power of words to utter, W. RALEGH. ('Letters,' pp. 161-163—endorsed by William Cecil, 2nd Earl of Salisbury: 'Sir Walter Ralegh's letters to my Father, touching the deathe of my Mother.')

CONTROVERSY.

Contentions among Professing Christians.

Certainly there is nothing more to be admired [= wondered at] and more to be lamented, than the private contentions, the passionate disputes, the personal hatred and the perpetual war, menaces and murders for religion among Christians; the discourse whereof hath so occupied the world as it hath well-near driven the practice thereof out of the world. Who would not soon resolve, that took knowledge but of the religious disputations among men and not of their lives which dispute, that there were no other thing in their desires than the purchase of heaven; and that the world itself were but used as it ought, and as an inn or place wherein to repose ourselves in passing on towards our celestial habitation? When, on the contrary, besides the discourse and outward profession, the soul hath nothing but hypocrisy. We are all (in effect) become comedians in religion, and while we act in gesture and voice divine virtues, in all the course of our lives we renounce our persons and the parts we play. For charity, justice and truth have but their being in terms, like the Philosopher's *materia prima*. Neither is it that wisdom which Solomon defineth to be the *schoolmasters of the knowledge of God*, that hath valuation in the world; it is enough that we give our good word; but the fame which is altogether exercised in the service of the world, as the gathering of riches chiefly, by which we purchase and obtain honours, with the many respects which attend it. (Preface, H. W.)

DUELLING AND PSEUDO-HONOUR.

Origin of the Duel.

After such time as Francis the French king upon some dispute about breach of faith, had sent the lie unto the emperor Charles the Fifth, thereby to draw him to a personal combat, every petty companion in France, in imitation of their master, made the giving of the lie mortality itself; holding it a matter of no small glory to have it said, that the meanest gentleman in France would not put up what the great emperor Charles the Fifth had patiently endured. From this beginning is derived a challenge of combat, grounded upon none of these occasions that were known to the ancients. For the honour of nations, the trial of right, the wager upon champions, or the objection and refutation of capital offences, are none of them nor all of them together, the argument of half so many duels as are founded upon mere private anger; yea or upon matter seeming worthy of anger in the opinion of the duellists. So that in these days, wherein every man takes unto himself a kingly liberty to offer, accept, and appoint personal combats, the giving of the lie, which ought to be the negation only in accusations for life, is become the most fruitful root of deadly quarrels. This is held a word so terrible and a charge so unpardonable, as will admit no other recompense than the blood of him that gives it. Thus the fashion, taken up in haste by the French gentlemen after the pattern of their king, is grown to be a custom, whence we have derived a kind of art and philosophy of quarrel, with certain grounds and rules, from whence the points of honour and the dependencies thereof are deduced. Yea there are (among many others no less ridiculous) some so mystical curiosities herein, as that it is held a far greater dishonour to receive from an enemy a slight touch with a cane than a sound blow with a sword; the one having relation to a slave, the other to a soldier. I confess that the difference is petty; though for mine own part, if I had had any such Italianated enemy in former times, I should willingly have made with him such an exchange, and have given him the point of honour to boot.

But let us examine indifferently [= unprejudicedly] the offence of this terrible word 'the *lie*,' with their conditions who are commonly of all others the moſt tender in receiving it. I ſay, that the moſt of thoſe who preſent death on the points of their ſwords to all that give it them, uſe nothing ſo much in their converſation and courſe of life, as to ſpeak and ſwear falſely. Yea, it is thereby that they ſhift and ſhuffle in the world and abuſe it; for how few are there among them, which, having aſſumed and ſworn to pay the monies and other things they borrow, do not break their word and promiſe as often as they engage it? Nay, how few are there among them that are not liars by record, by being ſued in ſome court or other of juſtice, upon breach of word or bond? For he which hath promiſed that he will pay money by a day, or promiſed anything elſe wherein he faileth, hath directly lied to him to whom the promiſe hath been made. Nay, what is the profeſſion of love that men make nowadays? What is the vowing of their service and of all they have, used in their ordinary compliments and in effect to every man whom they bid but good-morrow or salute, other than a courteous and court-like kind of lying? It is, saith a wise Frenchman (deriding therein the awful custom of his country), *un marché et complot fait ensemble se mocquer, mentir et piper les uns les autres,* 'a kind of merchandise and complot made among them, to revile, belie, and deride each other,' and so far nowadays in fashion and in use, as he that useth it not is accounted either dull or cynical. True it is, notwithstanding (omitting the old distinctions) that there is great difference between these mannerly and complimental lies, with those which are sometimes persuaded by necessity upon breach of promise and those which men use out of cowardice and fear, the latter confessing themselves to be in greater awe of man than of God, a vice of all others styled the most villainous. But now for 'the lie' itself, as it is made the subject of all our deadly quarrels in effect; to it I say that whoso gives another man the lie, when it is manifest that he hath lied, doth him no wrong at all, neither ought it to be more heinously taken than to tell him that he hath broken any promise which he hath otherwise made; for he that promiseth anything tells him to whom he hath promised that he will perform it, and in not performing it he hath made himself a liar. On the other side, he that gives any man the lie, when himself knows that he to whom it is given hath not lied, doth therein give the lie directly to himself. And what cause have I if I say that the sun shines when it doth shine, and that another fellow tells me I lie for it is midnight, to prosecute such an one to death for making himself a foolish ruffian and a liar in his own knowledge? For he that gives 'the lie' in any other dispute than in defence of his loyalty or life, gives it impertinently and ruffian-like. I will not deny but it is an extreme rudeness to tax [=accuse] any man in public with an untruth (if it be not pernicious and to his prejudice against whom the untruth is uttered), but all that is rude ought not to be civilized with death. That were more to admire and imitate a French custom and a wicked one, than to admire and to follow the counsel of God. (H. W., B. v., c. iii.)

Is it cowardice to refuse the duel?

But you will say these discourses [against duelling] favour of cowardice. It is true if you call it cowardice to fear God or hell, whereas he that is truly wise and truly valiant knows that there is nothing else to be feared. For against an enemy's sword we shall find ten thousand seven-penny men (waged at that price in the wars), that fear it as little, and perchance less, than any professed swordman in the world: *diligentissima in tutela sui fortitudo*, 'fortitude is a diligent preserver of itself.' 'It is,' saith Aristotle, 'a mediocrity between doubting and daring.' *Sicut non martyrem pœna; sic nec fortem pugna, sed causa:* 'as it is not the punishment that makes the martyr, so it is not the fighting that declares a valiant man; but fighting in a good cause.' In which whosoever shall resolvedly end his life, resolvedly in respect of the cause, to wit, in defence of his prince, religion, or country, as he may juſtly be numbered among the martyrs of God, ſo may thoſe that die with malicious hearts, in private combats, be called the martyrs of the devil. Neither do we, indeed, take our own revenge, or puniſh the injuries offered us, by the death of the injurious. For the true conqueſt of revenge is to give him of whom we would be revenged cauſe to repent him, and not to lay the repentance of another man's death on our own conſciences, *animaſque in vulnere ponere*, 'and to drown our ſouls in the wounds and blood of our enemies.' Therefore you will again aſk me if I condemn in generous and noble ſpirits the defence of their honours, being preſſed with injuries? I ſay that I do not if the injuries be violent; for the law of nature, which is a branch of the eternal law, and the laws of all Chriſtian kings and ſtates, do favour him that is aſſailed in the ſlaughter of his aſſailant. You will ſecondly aſk me whether a nobleman or a gentleman, being challenged by cartel by one of like quality, be not bound in point of honour to ſatisfy the challenge in private combat? I anſwer that he is not; becaufe (omitting the greateft, which is the point of honour) the point of the law is directly contrary and oppofite to that which they call the point of honour; the law which hath dominion over it, which can judge it, which can deftroy it; except you will ftyle thofe acts honourable where the hangman gives the garland, after feeing the laws of this land have appointed the hangman to fecond the conqueror and the laws of God appointed the devil to fecond the conquered, dying in malice; I fay that he is both bafe and a fool that accepts of any cartel fo accompanied. To this, perchance, it will be anfwered, that the kings of England and other Chriftian kings have feldom taken any fuch advantage over men of quality, but upon even terms have flain their private enemies. It is true that, as in times of trouble and combuftion, they have not often done it, fo did our noblemen and gentlemen in former ages, in all important injuries, fue unto the king to approve themfelves by battle and public combat. For as they dared not to brave the law fo did they difdain to fubmit themfelves to the fhameful revenge thereof, the same revenge (because it detesteth murder) that it hath declared against a common cutpurse or other thieves. Nay, let it be granted that a pardon be procured for such offenders, yet is not the manslayer freed by his pardon. For these two remedies hath the party grieved notwithstanding, that is to require justice by Grand Assize or by battle, upon his appeal, which suit, saith Sir Thomas Smith ('Commonwealth of England') is not denied; and he further saith (for I use his own words) 'that if the defendant (to wit, the manslayer) be convinced [= convicted], either by Great Assize or by battle, upon that appeal the manslayer shall die, notwithstanding the prince's pardon.' So favourable, saith the same learned gentleman, are 'our prince and the law of our realm to justice and to the punishment of blood violently shed.' It may further be demanded how our noblemen and gentlemen shall be reputed in honour where an enemy taking the start, either in words or blows, shall lay on them an infamy insufferable? I say that a marshall's court will easily give satisfaction in both. (H. W., B. v., c. iii.)

EASTERN POSITION.

Now becaufe Paradife was reached by Mofes towards the Eaft, thence came the cuftom of praying towards the Eaft, and not by inftitution of the Chaldeans; and therefore all our churches are built Eaft and Weft, as to the point where the fun rifeth in March, which is directly over Paradife, faith Damafcenus, affirming that we always pray towards the Eaft as looking towards Paradife, whence we were caft out; and yet the temple of Solomon had their priefts and fcribes which turned themfelves in their fervice and divine ceremonies always towards the Weft, thereby to avoid the fuperftition of the Egyptians and Chaldeans. But becaufe Eaft and Weft are but in refpect of places (for although Paradife was Eaft from Judea, yet it was Weft from Perfia), and the ferving of God is everywhere in the world, the matter is not great which way we turn our faces, fo our hearts ftand right, other than this that we all dwell Weft from Paradife, and pray, turning ourfelves to the Eaft, may remember thereby to befeech God that as by Adam's fall we have loft the Paradife on earth, so by Christ's death and passion we may be made partakers of the Paradise Celestial and the Kingdom of Heaven. (H. W., B. i., c. iii.)

EPITAPHS.

Epitaph on the Earl of Salisbury, died May 24, 1612.

Here lies Hobbinol, our pastor whilere,
That once in a quarter our fleeces did shear;
To fleece us his cur he kept under clog,
And was ever after both shepherd and dog.
For oblation to Pan his custom was thus:
He first gave a trifle, then offered up us;
And through his false worship such fines he did gain,
As kept him o' th' mountain and us on the plain;
Where many a hornpipe he tuned to his Phyllis,
And sweetly sang Walsingham to's Amaryllis.*

* See our Introduction.

Epitaph on the Earl of Leicester, died September 4, 1588.

Here lies the noble warrior that never blunted fword;
Here lies the noble courtier that never kept his word;
Here lies his excellency that govern'd all the State;
Here lies the Lord of Leicefter that all the world did hate.

PORTRAITS OF QUEEN ELIZABETH.

I could fay much more of the king's majefty [James I.] without flattery, did I not fear the imputation of prefumption, and withal fufpect, that it might befall thefe papers of mine (though the lofs were little) as it did the pictures of Queen Elizabeth, made by unfkilful and common painters; which, by her own commandment, were knocked in pieces, and caft into the fire. For ill artifts, in fetting out the beauty of the external, and weak writers, in defcribing the virtues of the internal, do often leave to posterity, of well-formed faces a deformed memory, and of the most perfect and princely minds a most defective representation. (Preface, H. W.)

EQUIVOCATION.

If it be permitted, by the help of a ridiculous distinction, or by a God-mocking equivocation, to swear one thing by the name of the living God and to reserve in silence a contrary intent; the life of men, the estates of men, the faith of subjects to kings, of servants to their masters, of vassals to their lords, of wives to their husbands, and of children to their parents, and of all trials of right, will not only be made uncertain, but all the chains whereby freemen are tied in the world, be torn asunder. It is by oath, when kings and armies cannot pass, that we enter into the cities of our enemies, and into their armies. It is by oath that wars take end which weapons cannot end. And what is it, or ought it to be, that makes an oath

thus powerful but this, that he that
sweareth by the name of God doth assure
others that his words are true as the
Lord of all the world is true, whom he
calleth for a witness and in whose
presence he that taketh the oath hath
promised? I am not ignorant of these
poor evasions, which play with the
severity of God's commandments in this
land; but this indeed is the best answer,
that he breaks no faith that hath none to
break, for whosoever hath faith and the
fear of God dare not do it. (H. W.)

THE EARL OF ESSEX, 1600.

To Sir Robert Cecil.

Sir,—I am not wise enough to give you
advice, but if you take it for a good
counsel to relent towards this tyrant,
you will repent it when it shall be too
late. His malice is fixed and will not
evaporate by any your mild courses.
For he will ascribe the alteration to her
Majesty's pusillanimity and not to your
good nature, knowing that you work but
upon her humour and not out of any

love to him. The less you make him, the less he shall be able to harm you and yours. And if her Majesty's favour fail him, he will again decline to a common person.

For after-revenges, fear them not; for your own father that was esteemed to be the contriver of Norfolk's ruin, yet his son followeth your father's son and loveth him. Humours of men succeed not [= not inherited], but grow by occasions and accidents of time and power. Somerset made no revenge on the Duke of Northumberland's heirs. Northumberland that now is thinks not of Hatton's issue. Kellaway lives that murdered the brother of Horsey, and Horsey let him go bye all his lifetime.

I could name you a thousand of those; and therefore after-fears are but prophesies, or rather conjectures, for causes remote. Look to the present and you do wisely. His son shall be the youngest Earl of England but one, and if his father be now kept down William Cecil shall be able to keep as many men at his heels as he, and more, too. He may also match in a better house than his; and so their fear is not worth the fearing. But if the father continue, he will be able to break the branches and pull up the tree, root and all. Lose not your advantage; if you do I read your destiny. Yours to the end, W. RALEGH.

Let the Queen hold Bothwell while she hath him. He will ever be the canker of her estate and safety. Princes are lost by security, and preserved by prevention. I have seen the last of her good days and all ours after his liberty. ('Letters,' pp. 222, 223; see Edwards, vol. i., pp. 258, 259; vol. ii., pp. 213-221; and our Introduction.)

FAME.

To these undertakings the greatest lords of the world have been stirred up rather by the desire of fame, which plougheth up the air and soweth in the wind, than by the affection of bearing rule, which draweth after it so much vexation and so many cares. And that this is true the good advice of Cineas to

Pyrrhus proves. And certainly, as fame hath often been dangerous to the living, so is it to the dead of no use at all, because separate from knowledge. Which were it obtained, and the extreme ill bargain of buying this lasting discourse understood by them which are dissolved, they themselves would then rather have wished to have stolen out of the world without noise, than to be put in mind that they have purchased the report of their actions in the world by rapine, oppression and cruelty; by giving in spoil the innocent and labouring soul to the idle and insolent, and by having emptied the cities of the world of their ancient inhabitants and filled them again with so many and so variable sorrows. (H. W., B. v., c. vi.)

FAREWELL LETTERS.

On being Sentenced to Death. To Lady Ralegh, July, 1603.

Receive from thy unfortunate husband these his last lines; these the last words that ever thou shalt receive from him.

That I can live never to see thee and my child more, I cannot. I have defired God and difputed with my reafon, but nature and compaffion hath the victory. That I can live to think how you are both left a fpoil to my enemies, and that my name fhall be a difhonour to my child, I cannot. I cannot endure the memory thereof. Unfortunate woman! unfortunate child! comfort yourfelves; truft God and be contented with your poor eftate. I would have bettered it if I had enjoyed a few years.

Thou art a young woman, and forbear not to marry again. It is now nothing to me. Thou art no more mine, nor I thine. So witnefs that thou didft love me once, take care that thou marry not to pleafe fenfe, but to avoid poverty and to preferve thy child. That thou didft alfo love me living, witnefs it to others to my poor daughter, to whom I have given nothing: for his fake who will be cruel to himfelf to preferve thee. Be charitable to her and teach thy fon to love her for his father's fake.

For myfelf, I am left of all men that have done good to many. All good turns forgotten, all my errors revived and expounded to all extremity of ill. All my services, hazards and expenses for my country — plantings, discoveries, fights, counsels, and whatsoever else — malice hath covered over. I am now made an enemy and traitor by the word of an unworthy man. He hath proclaimed me to be a partaker of his vain imaginations, notwithstanding the whole course of my life hath approved the contrary, as my death shall approve it. Woe, woe, woe be unto him by whose falsehood we are lost! He hath separated us asunder. He hath slain my honour, my fortune. He hath robbed thee of thy husband, thy child of his father, and me of you both. O God! thou dost know my wrongs. Know, then, thou my wife and child; know, then, thou my lord and king, that I ever thought them too honest to betray and too good to conspire against.

But, my wife, forgive them all, as I do. Live humble, for thou hast but a time also. God forgive my Lord Harry [Howard], for he was my heavy enemy. And for my Lord Cecil, I thought he would never forsake me in extremity.

I would not have done it him, God knows. But do not thou know it, for he muſt be maſter of thy child [as Maſter of the Court of Wards], and may have compaſſion of him. Be not diſmayed that I died in deſpair of God's mercies. Strive not to diſpute it. But aſſure thyſelf that God hath not left me nor Satan tempted me. Hope and Deſpair live not together. I know it is forbidden to deſtroy ourſelves, but I truſt it is forbidden in this ſort, that we deſtroy not ourſelves deſpairing of God's mercy. The mercy of God is immeaſurable; the cogitations of men comprehend it not.

In the Lord I have ever truſted; and I know that my Redeemer liveth. Far is it from me to be tempted unto Satan; I am only tempted unto Sorrow, whoſe ſharp teeth devour my heart. O God! Thou art goodneſs itſelf! Thou canſt not but be good to me! O God! Thou art mercy itſelf! Thou canſt not but be merciful to me!

For my eſtate, it is conveyed to feoffees, to your couſin Brett and others. I leave but a bare eſtate for a ſhort life. My plate is at gage in Lombard Street:

my debts are many. To Peter Vanlove
I owe £600. To Antrobus as much,
but Compton is to pay £300 of it. To
Michael Hickes £100. To George Carew
£100. To Nicholas Sanderson £100.
To John Fitzjames £100. To Master
Waddon £100. To a poor man, one
Hawkes, for horses £70. To a poor
man called Hunt £20. Take first care
of those, for God's sake. To a brewer
at Weymouth, and a baker for Lord
Cecil's ship and mine, I think £80.
John Reynolds knoweth it. And let
that poor man have his true part of my
return from Virginia. And let the poor
men's wages be paid with the goods, for
the Lord's sake. Oh, what will my poor
servants think at their return, when they
hear I am accused to be Spanish, who
sent them, at my great charge, to plant
and discover upon his territory!

Oh, intolerable infamy! O God! I
cannot resist these thoughts. I cannot
live to think how I am derided, to think
of the expectation of my enemies, the
scorns I shall receive, the cruel words of
lawyers, the infamous taunts and despites,
to be made a wonder and a spectacle!
O Death! hasten thou unto me, that

thou mayest destroy the memory of these and lay me up in dark forgetfulness. O Death! destroy my memory, which is my tormentor; my thoughts and my life cannot dwell in one body. But do thou forget me, poor wife, that thou mayest live to bring up my poor child.

 I recommend unto you my poor brother Adrian Gilbert. The lease of Sandridge is his, and none of mine. Let him have it, for God's cause. He knows what is due to me upon it. And be good to Kemish, for he is a perfect honest man and hath much wrong for my sake. For the rest, I commend me to them and them to God. And the Lord knows my sorrow to part from thee and my poor child. But part I must, by enemies and injuries; part with shame and triumph of my detractors. And therefore be contented with this work of God, and forget me in all things but thine own honour and the love of mine.

 I bless my poor child, and let him know his father was no traitor. Be bold of my innocence; for God, to Whom I offer life and soul, knows it. And whosoever thou choose again after me, let him be but thy politique hufband. But let my fon be thy beloved; for he is part of me, and I live in him; and the difference is but in the number and not in the kind. And the Lord for ever keep thee and them, and give thee comfort in both worlds. (Without fignature or addrefs. 'Letters,' pp. 383-387. See our Introduction.)

Letter of Farewell and Confolation to Lady Ralegh, on the eve of his expected execution, December, 1603.

You fhall receive, dear wife, my laft words in thefe my laft lines. My love I fend you that you may keep it when I am dead, and my counfel that you may remember it when I am no more. I would not, with my laft will, prefent you with forrows, dear Befs. Let them go to the grave with me and be buried in the duft. And feeing it is not the will of God that ever I fhall fee you in this life, bear my deftruction gently and with a heart like yourfelf.

Firft, I fend you all the thanks my

heart may conceive or my pen exprefs, for your many troubles and cares taken for me, which—though they have not taken effect as you wifhed—yet my debt is to you never the lefs ; but pay it I never fhall in this world.

Secondly, I befeech you, for the love you bore me living, that you do not hide yourfelf many days, but by your travel feek to help your miferable fortunes and the right of your poor children. Your mourning cannot avail me that am but duft.

You fhall underftand that my lands were conveyed to my child *bonâ-fide*. The writings were drawn at Midfummer was twelve months, as divers can witnefs. My honeft coufin Brett can teftify fo much, and Dalberie, too, can remember fomewhat therein. And I truft my blood will quench their malice that defire my flaughter ; and that they will not alfo feek to kill you and yours with extreme poverty. To what friend to direct thee I know not, for all mine have left me in the true time of trial ; and I plainly perceive that my death was determined from the firft day. Moft forry I am (as God knoweth) that being thus surprised with death, I can leave you no better estate. I meant you all mine office of wines or that I could purchase by selling it; half my stuff and jewels, but some few for my boy. But God hath prevented all my determinations: the great God that worketh all in all. If you can live free from want, care for no more; for the rest is but vanity. Love God and begin betimes to repose yourself on Him; therein shall you find true and lasting riches and endless comfort. For the rest, when you have travailed and wearied your thoughts on all sorts of worldly cogitations, you shall sit down by sorrow in the end. Teach your son also to serve and fear God while he is young, that the fear of God may grow up in him. Then will God be a husband unto you and a father unto him; a husband and a father which can never be taken from you.

Bayley oweth me £200 and Adrian £600. In Jersey also I have much owing me. The arrears of the wines will pay my debts. And, howsoever, for my soul's health, I beseech you pay all poor men. When I am gone no doubt you shall be sought unto by many, for the world thinks that I am very rich; but take heed of the pretences of men and of their affections, for they last but in honest and worthy men. And no greater misery can befall you in this life than to become a prey, and afterwards to be despised. I speak it (God knows) not to dissuade you from marriage—for that will be best for you—both in respect of God and the world. As for me, I am no more yours nor you mine. Death hath cut us asunder, and God hath divided me from the world and you from me.

Remember your poor child for his father's sake, that comforted you and loved you in his happiest times.

Get those letters (if it be possible) which I writ to the Lords, wherein I sued for my life; but God knoweth that it was for you and yours that I desired it; but it is true that I disdain myself for begging it. And know it (dear wife) that your son is the child of a true man, and who, in his own respect, despiseth Death and all his misshapen and ugly forms.

I cannot write much. God knows

how hardly I ſtole this time when all ſleep; and it is time to ſeparate my thoughts from the world. Beg my dead body, which living was denied you; and either lay it at Sherburne, if the land continue, or in Exeter Church by my father and mother. I can write no more. Time and Death call me away.

The everlaſting, infinite, powerful and inſcrutable God, that Almighty God that is goodneſs itſelf, mercy itſelf, the true life and light, keep you and yours, and have mercy on me and teach me to forgive my perſecutors and falſe accuſers; and ſend us to meet in His glorious kingdom. My true wife farewell. Bleſs my poor boy; pray for me. My true God hold you both in His arms. Written with the dying hand of, ſometime thy huſband, but now (alas!) overthrown, yours that was but now not my own, W. RALEGH. ('Letters,' pp. 284-287. See our Introduction.)

FATE AND FREE WILL.

Influence of the stars.

Certainly it cannot be doubted but the Stars are inftruments of far greater ufe than to give an obfcure light, and for man to gaze on after funfet; it being manifeft that the diverfity of feafons, the Winters and Summers, more hot and cold, are not fo uncertained by the fun and moon alone, who always keep one and the fame courfe, but that the ftars have alfo their work therein. And if we cannot deny but that God hath given virtues to fprings and fountains, to cold earth to plants and ftones and minerals, why fhould we rob the beautiful ftars of their working powers? For feeing they are many in number, and of eminent beauty and magnitude, we may not think that in the treafury of His wifdom which is infinite, there can be wanting (even for every ftar) a peculiar virtue and operation; as every herb, plant, fruit, and flower adorning the face of the earth hath the like. For as thefe were not created to beautify the earth alone, and to cover and fhadow her dusty face, but otherwise for the use of man and beast, to feed them and cure them; so were not these uncountable glorious bodies set in the firmament, to no other end than to adorn it, but for instruments and organs of His Divine Providence, so far as it hath pleased His just will to determine. (H. W., B. i., c. i.)

Fate.

As of Nature such is the dispute and contention concerning Fate or Destiny; of which the opinion of those learned men that have written thereof may be safely received, had they not thereunto annexed and fastened an inevitable necessity and made it more general and universally powerful than it is, by giving it dominion over the mind of man and over his will, of which Ovid and Juvenal:

> *Ratio fatum vincere nulla valet.*
> *Servis regna dabunt, captivis fata triumphos.*
> 'Gainst Fate no counsel can prevail:
> Kingdoms to slaves by Destiny,
> To captives triumphs given be.
> [Ovid's Tristia, iii. vi. 18; Juvenal, vii. 201.]

Sir Walter Raleigh.

An error of the Chaldeans, and after them of the Stoics, the Pharisees, Pricillianists, the Bardisanists, and others, as Basil, Augustine, and Thomas have showed, but that Fate is an obedience of second causes to the first was well conceived of Hermes and Apuleius, the Platonist. . . . But in this question of Fate the middle course is to be followed; that as with the heathen we do not bind God to His creatures in this supposed necessity of destiny; so, on the contrary, we do not rob those beautiful creatures of their powers and offices [*i.e.*, the stars]. For had any of these second causes despoiled God of His prerogative, or had God Himself constrained the mind and will of man to impious acts by any celestial enforcements, then sure the impious excuse of some were justifiable of whom St. Augustine: 'Where we reprehend them of evil deeds, they again with wicked perverseness urge that rather the author and creator of the stars than the doer of the evil, is to be accused' (20 supr. Gen. ad lit.). (H. W., B. i., c. i.)

Astrology.

But there is nothing (after God's reserved power) that so much setteth this art of influence out of square and rule as education doth, for there are none in the world so wickedly inclined but that a religious instruction and bringing up may fashion anew and reform them; nor any so well-disposed whom (the reins being let loose) the continual fellowship and familiarity and the examples of dissolute men, may not corrupt and deform. Vessels will ever retain a favour of their first liquor; it being equally difficult either to cleanse the mind once corrupted or to extinguish the sweet savours of virtue first received, when the mind was yet tender, open and easily seasoned; but where a favourable constellation (allowing that the stars incline the will) and a virtuous education do happily arrive, or the contrary in both, thereby it is that men are found so exceeding virtuous or vicious, heaven and earth (as it were) running together and agreeing in one; for as the seeds of virtue may, by the art and husbandry of Christian counsel, produce better and more beautiful fruit than the strength of self-nature and kind could have yielded them; so the plants, apt to grow wild and to change themselves into weeds, by being set in a soil suitable and like themselves, are made more unsavoury and filled with poison. It was, therefore, truly affirmed: 'A wise man assisteth the work of the stars, as the husbandman helpeth the nature of the soil.' And Ptolemy confesseth thus much: 'A wise man, and the ominous art of a wise physician, shall prevail against the stars.' Lastly, we ought all to know that God created the stars as He did the rest of the universe, whose influences may be called His reserved and unwritten laws. . . . But let us consider how they bind. . . . It were then impious to take that power and liberty from God Himself which His substitutes [kings] enjoy. . . . God (which only knoweth the operation of His own creatures truly) hath assured us that there is no inclination or temptation so forcible which our humble prayers and desires may not make frustrate and break asunder; for were it (as the Stoics conceive) that Fate or

Destiny, though depending upon eternal power, yet being once ordered and disposed, had such a connection and immutable dependency, that God Himself should in a kind have shut up Himself therein, 'How miserable then were the condition of men,' saith St. Augustine, 'left altogether without hope!' And if this strength of the stars were so transferred as that God had quitted unto them all dominion over His creatures; be he Pagan or Christian that so believeth, the only true God of the one and the imaginary God of the other, would thereby be despoiled of all worship, reverence, or respect. And certainly God which hath promised us the reward of well-doing, which Christ Himself claimed at the hands of the Father ('I have finished the work which Thou gavest Me to do') [St. John xviii. 4], and the same God who hath threatened unto us the sorrow and torment of offences, could not, contrary to His merciful nature, be so unjust as to bind us inevitably to the destinies or influences of the stars, or subject our souls to any imposed necessity. But it was well said of Plotinus, that the stars were significant but not efficient, giving them yet something less than their due; and therefore as I do not consent with those who would make those glorious creatures of God virtueless, so I think that we derogate from His eternal and absolute power and providence, to ascribe to them the same dominion over our immortal souls, which they have over all bodily substances and perishable matters; for the souls of men loving and fearing God, receive influence from that Divine light itself, whereof the sun's clarity and that of the stars is by Plato called but a shadow : 'Light is the shadow of God's brightness, who is the light of lights' (Pol. 6, Ficinus in l. 7, pol.). (H. W., B. i., c. i.)

GEOGRAPHY.

Fictions of Maps—a ' Pretty Jest.'

The fictions, or let them be called conjectures, painted on maps, do serve only to mislead such discoverers as rashly believe them, drawing upon the publishers either some angry curses or well-deserved scorn ; but to keep their own credit, they cannot serve always. To which purpose I remember a pretty jest of Don Pedro de Sarmiento, a worthy Spanish gentleman who had been employed by his king in planting a colony upon the Straits of Magellan: for when I asked him, being then my prisoner, some questions about an island in those straits, which methought might have done either benefit or displeasure to his enterprise, he told me merrily, that it was to be called the Painter's Wife's Island; saying that whilst the fellow drew this map, his wife sitting by desired him to put in one country for her, that she in imagination might have an island of her own. But in filling up the blanks of old histories, we need not to be so scrupulous. For it is not to be feared that Time should run backward and by restoring the things themselves to knowledge, make our conjectures appear ridiculous. What if some good copy of an ancient author could be found, showing (if we have it not already) the perfect truth of these uncertainties? Would it be more shame to have believed in the meanwhile Annius or Terniellus than to have believed nothing? (H. W., B. ii., c. xxiii.)

GREAT MEN.

A Reverend Respect for Great Men.

But you will say that there are some things else, and of greater regard than gathering of riches . . . as the reverend respect that is held of great men and the honour done unto them by all sort of people. And it is true indeed, provided that an inward love for their justice and piety accompany the outward worship given to their places and power; without which what is the applause of the multitude, but as the outcry of an herd of animals, who, without the knowledge of any true cause, please themselves with the noise they make? For seeing it is a thing exceeding rare to distinguish virtue and fortune, the most impious, if prosperous, have ever been applauded; the most virtuous, if unprosperous, have ever been despised. For as Fortune's man rides the horse, so Fortune herself rides the man; who, when he is defcended and on foot, the man taken from his beaft and fortune from the man, a bafe groom beats the one and a bitter contempt fpurns the other with equal liberty. (Preface, H. W.)

GOD—CREATION—PROVIDENCE.

Creation and Providence.

The examples of Divine Providence everywhere found (the firft Divine hiftories being nothing elfe but a continuation of fuch examples) have perfuaded me to fetch my beginning from the beginning of all things, to wit, Creation. For though thefe two glorious actions of the Almighty be fo near—as it were, linked together—that the one necef-farily completes the other, Creation inferring Providence (for what father forfaketh the child that he hath begotten?), and Providence prefuppofing Creation ; yet many of thofe that have feemed to excel in worldly wifdom have gone about to disjoin the coherence: the Epicure [=Epicurean] denying both Creation and Providence, but granting that the world had a beginning; the Aristotelian granting Providence, but denying both the Creation and the beginning. (*Ibid.*)

By Faith Creation is Understood.

Now, although this doctrine of FAITH touching the Creation in time (for 'by *faith* we understand that the world was made by the Word of God' [Hebrews xi. 3]) be too weighty a work for Aristotle's rotten ground to bear up, upon which he hath notwithstanding founded the defences and fortresses of all his verbal doctrine; yet that the necessity of infinite power and the world's beginning, and the impossibility of the contrary even in the judgment of natural reason wherein he believed, had not better informed him, it is greatly to be marvelled at. And it is no less strange that those men which are desirous of knowledge (seeing Aristotle hath failed in this main point, and taught little other than terms in the rest) have so retrenched their minds from the following and overtaking of truth, and so absolutely subjected themselves to the law of those philosophical principles, as all contrary kind of teaching in the search of causes they have condemned either for fantastical or curious. But doth it follow that the positions of heathen philosophers are undoubted grounds and principles indeed because so called? or that, *ipsi dixerunt*, doth make them to be such? Certainly no. But this is true, that where natural reason hath built anything so strong against itself, as the same reason can hardly assail it, much less batter it down; the same in every question of Nature and finite power may be approved for a fundamental law of human knowledge. For saith Charron in his Book of Wisdom, *Toute proposition humaine a autant d'authorité que l'autre, si la raison n'on fait la difference*, 'Every human proposition hath equal authority, if reason make not the difference,' the rest being but the fables of principles. But hereof how shall the upright and impartial judgment of man give a sentence where opposition and examination are not admitted to give us evidence? And to this purpose it was well said of Lactantius (De Orig. Erroris, l. 2, c. viii.): 'They neglect their own wisdom who, without any judgment, approve the invention of those that forewent them, and suffer themselves, after the manner of beasts, to be led by them.' By the advantage of which sloth and dulness, ignorance is now become so powerful a tyrant as it hath set true philosophy, physic, and divinity in a pillory, and written over the first, *Contra negantem principia;* over the second, *Virtus specifica;* and over the third, *Ecclesia Romana.* (*Ibid.*)

Aristotle on Creation condemned.

But, for myself, I shall never be persuaded that God hath shut up all light of learning within the lantern of Aristotle's brains, or that it was ever said unto him as unto Esdras, *Accendam in corde tuo lucernam intellectus;* that God hath given invention but to the heathen, and that they only have invaded Nature, and found the strength and bottom thereof; the same Nature having consumed all her store, and left nothing of price to after-ages. That these and those be the causes of these and those effects, time hath taught us, and not reason; and so hath experience without art. The cheese-wife knoweth it as well as the philosopher, that sour rennet doth coagulate her milk into a curd. But if we ask a reason of this cause, why the sourness doth it? whereby it doth it? and the manner how? I think that there is nothing to be found in vulgar philosophy to satisfy this and many other like vulgar questions. But man, to cover his ignorance in the least things, who cannot give a true reason for the grass under his feet why it should be green rather than red or of any other colour; that could never yet discover the way and reason of Nature's working in those which are far less noble creatures than himself, who is far more noble than the heavens themselves; 'Man,' saith Solomon, 'that can hardly discern the things that are upon the earth, and with great labour find out the things that are before us' (i. 9); that hath so short a time in the world, as he no sooner begins to learn than to die; that hath in his memory but borrowed knowledge; in his understanding nothing truly; that is ignorant of the essence of his own soul, and which the wisest of the Naturalists (if Aristotle be he) could never so much as define but by the action and effect, telling us what it works (which all men know as well as he), but not what it is, which neither he nor any else doth know but God that created it ('For though I were perfect, yet I know not my soul,' saith Job [ix. 21]); man, I say, that is but an idiot in the next cause of his own life, and in the cause of all the actions of his life, will, notwithstanding, examine the art of God in creating the world; of God 'Who,' saith Job, 'is so excellent as we know Him not' (xxxvii. 23); and examine the beginning of being. (*Ibid.*)

Secondary Causes.

Man will disable God's power to make a world without matter to make it of. He will rather give the motes of the air for a cause; cast the work on necessity or chance; bestow the honour thereof on Nature; make two powers, the one to be the author of the matter, the other of the form; and lastly, for want of a workman, have it eternal; which latter opinion Aristotle, to make himself the author of a new doctrine, brought into the world, and his sectators have maintained it. (*Ibid.*)

God by Necessity of Invincible Reason.

Parati ac conjurati quos sequuntur, philosophorum animus invictis opiniones tueri. For Hermes, who lived at once with or soon after Moses, Zoroaster, Musæus, Orpheus, Linus, Anaximines, Anaxagoras, Empedocles, Melissus, Pherecydes, Thales, Cleanthes, Pythagoras, Plato, and many others (whose opinions are exquisitely gathered by Steuchius Eugubinus), found, in the necessity of invincible reason, One eternal and infinite Being to be the parent of the universal. 'All these men's opinions,' saith Lactantius (5), 'though uncertain, come to this, that they agree upon one Providence; whether the same be Nature, or light, or reason, or understanding, or destiny, or Divine ordinance, that it is the same which we call God.' Certainly, as all the rivers in the world, though they have divers risings and divers runnings; though they sometimes hide themselves for a while under ground, and seem to be lost in sea-like lakes, do at last find and fall into the great ocean, so, after all the searches that human capacity hath, and after all philosophical contemplation and curiosity, in the necessity of this Infinite Power all the reason of man ends and dissolves itself. (*Ibid.*)

Out of Nothing Nothing: Sufficient Cause Sufficient Effect.

Now for those who from that ground 'That out of nothing nothing is made,' infer the world's eternity; and yet not so savage [= heathen] therein as those are which give an eternal being to dead matter; it is true, if the word 'nothing' be taken in the affirmative, and the making imposed upon natural agents and finite power, that out of nothing nothing is made. But seeing their great doctor, Aristotle himself, confesseth 'That all the ancients decree a kind of beginning, and the same to be infinite,' and a little after, more largely and plainly (Steuc. Eug., l. 3, c. 9., and Arist. Phys., iii., 20), it is strange that this philosopher, with his followers, should rather make choice out of falsehood to conclude falsely, than out of truth to resolve truly. For if we compare the world universal and all the immeasurable orbs of heaven and those marvellous bodies of the sun, moon and stars, with *ipsum infinitum*, it may truly be said of them all, which himself affirmeth of his imagining *materia prima*, that they are neither *quid, quale*, nor *quantum;* and, therefore, to bring finite (which hath no proportion with infinite) out of infinite (*qui destruit omnem proportionem*) is no work in God's power. And, therefore, Anaximander, Melissus and Empedocles call the world universal; but *particulam universitatis et infinitatis*, 'a parcel of that which is the universality and the infinity itself'; and Plato, but 'a shadow of God.' But the other, to prove the world's eternity, urgeth this maxim, that 'a sufficient and effectual cause being granted an answerable effect thereof is also granted'; inferring that God being for ever a sufficient and effectual cause of the world, the effect of the cause should also have been for ever, to wit the world universal. But what a strange mockery is this in so great a master, to confess a sufficient and effectual cause of the world (to wit, an Almighty God) in His antecedent and the same God to be a God restrained in His conclusion; to make God free in power and bound in will; able to effect, unable to determine; able to make all things, and yet unable to make choice of the time when; for this were impiously to resolve of God as of natural necessity, which hath neither choice nor will, nor understanding; which cannot but work, matter being present, as fire, to burn things combustible. (*Ibid.*)

The Pattern of Creation Eternal.

To this anfwer (as before) in itfelf fufficient, others add further, that the pattern or image of the world may be faid to be eternal, which the Platonicks call *fpiritualem mundum*, and do in this fort diftinguifh the idea and creation in time, 'That reprefentative or the intentional world,' fay they, 'the fampler of the vifible world, the firft work of God, was equally ancient with the architect; for it was for ever with Him, and ever fhall be. This material world, the fecond work or creature of God, doth differ from the worker in this, that it was not from everlafting; and in this it doth agree, that it fhall be for ever to come.' The firft point, That it was not for ever, all Chriftians confefs: the other they underftand no otherwife than that after the confummation of this world, there fhall be 'a new heaven and a new earth' without any new creation of matter. But of thefe things we need not here ftand to argue, though fuch opinions be not unworthy the propounding; in this confideration of an eternal unchangeable Cause producing a changeable and temporal effect. (*Ibid.*)

Creation without Ending.

But to return to them which, denying that ever the world had any beginning, withal deny that ever it shall have any end; and to this purpose affirm that it was never heard, never read, never seen, nor not by any reason perceived, that the heavens have suffered corruption; or that they appear any way the elder by continuance, or in any sort otherwise than they were; which, had they been subject to final corruption, some change would have been discerned in so long a time; to this it is answered, that the little change as yet perceived doth rather prove their newness, and that they have not continued so long, than that they will continue for ever as they are. And if conjectural arguments may receive answer by conjectures, it then seemeth that some alteration may be found. For either Aristotle (Met. 2), Pliny (l. 2, c. 8), Strabo (l. 3), Beda

(De ratione tem. ii., c. 32), Aquinas (i. p. q. 102, art. 2), and others, were grossly mistaken; or else those parts of the world lying within the burnt zone were not in olden times habitable, by reason of the sun's heat; neither were the seas under the equinoctial navigable. But we know by experience that those regions so situate are filled with people and exceeding temperate; and the sea over which we navigate, passable enough. We read also many histories of deluges, and how that in the time of Phaeton divers places in the world were burnt up by the sun's violent heat. (*Ibid.*)

Alterations in Creation.

But in a word, this observation is exceeding feeble. For we know it for certain that stone walls, of matter mouldering and feeble, have stood two or three thousand years, and that many things have been dragged up out of the earth, of that depth as supposed to have been buried by the General Flood, without any alteration either of substance or figure; yea it is believed, and it is very probable, that the gold which is daily found in mines and rocks under ground, was created together with the earth. And if bodies elementary and compounded, the eldest times have not invaded and corrupted, what great alteration should we look for in celestial and quintessential bodies? And yet we have reason to think that the sun, by whose help all creatures are generate, doth not in these latter ages assist nature as heretofore. We have neither giants such as the eldest world had, nor mighty men such as the elder world had, but all things in general are reported of less virtue which from the heavens receive virtue. Whence, if the nature of a Preface would permit a larger discourse, we might easily fetch store of proof, as that this world shall at length have end as that once it had beginning. (*Ibid.*)

Creation not Self-existing.

Who was it that appointed the earth to keep the centre, and gave order that it should hang in the air; that the sun should travel between the tropics, and never exceed those bounds, nor fail to perform that progress once in every year; the moon to live by borrowed light; the fixed stars (according to common opinion) to be fastened like nails in a cart wheel, and the planets to wander at their pleasure? Or, if none of these had power over other, was it out of charity and love that the sun, by his perpetual travel within those two arches, hath visited, given light unto and relieved all parts of the earth and the countries therein, by turns and times? Out of doubt, if the sun have of his own accord kept this course in all eternity, he may justly be called eternal charity and everlasting love. The same may be said of all the stars, who, being all of them most large and clear fountains of virtue and operation, may also be called eternal virtues; the earth may be called eternal patience; the moon an eternal borrower and beggar; and man, of all other, the most miserable, eternally mortal. And what were this but to believe again in the old play of the gods? yea, in more gods by millions than ever Hesiod dreamt of. But instead of this mad folly, we see it well enough with our feeble and mortal eyes, and the eyes of our reason discern it better, that the sun, moon, stars and the earth, are limited, bounded and constrained; themselves they have not constrained, nor could. (*Ibid.*)

That the Invisible God is seen in His Creatures.

God, Whom the wisest men acknowledge to be a Power ineffable and virtue infinite; a Light by abundant clarity invisible; an Understanding which Itself can only comprehend; an Essence eternal and spiritual, of absolute pureness and simplicity; was and is pleased to make Himself known by the work of the world: in the wonderful magnitude whereof (all which He embraceth, filleth and sustaineth) we behold the image of that glory which cannot be measured, and withal, that One and yet universal Nature which cannot be defined. In the glorious lights of heaven we perceive a shadow of His Divine countenance; in His merciful provision for all that live, His manifold goodness; and lastly, in creating and making existent the world universal, by the absolute art of His own word, His power and almightiness: which power, light, virtue, wisdom and goodness, being all but attributes of One simple essence and One God, we in all admire and in part discern *per speculum creaturarum*, that is, in the disposition, order and variety of celestial and terrestrial bodies: terrestrial, in their strange and manifold diversities; celestial, in their beauty and magnitude; which in their continual and contrary motions, are neither repugnant, intermixed, nor confounded. By these potent effects we approach to the knowledge of the Omnipotent Cause, and by these motions, their Almighty Mover. (H. W., B. i., c. i.)

'*Feeling after God.*'

There is not anything in this world of more efficacy and force to allure and draw to it the hearts of men than God, which is the *summum bonum*. He is carefully desired and continually sought for of all creatures; for all regard Him as their last end and refuge. Light things apply themselves upwards, heavy things downwards; the heavens to revolution, the herbs to flowers, trees to bear fruit, beasts to preserve their kind, and man in seeking his tranquility and everlasting glory. But forasmuch as God is of so high a nature as the sense and understanding of man cannot conceive it, every man directly turns himself to that place where He leaves some print of His power, and declares some sign of His existence; and to such persons to whom He seemeth more especially to have revealed Himself. ('Cities.')

God Inconceivable.

'There would be no difference between God and man if man's understanding could conceive the counsels and disposing of that eternal Majesty' (Lactantius in Præf.); and therefore to be over-curious in searching how the

all-powerful Word of God wrought in
the creation of the world, or His all-
piercing and operative Spirit diftinguifh-
ing, gave form to the matter of the
univerfal, is a labour and fearch like
unto his who, not contented with a
known and fafe ford, will prefume to
pafs over the greateft river in all parts
where he is ignorant of their depths;
for fo doth the one lofe his life and the
other his underftanding. We behold
the fun, and enjoy his light, as long as
we look towards it but tenderly and
circumfpectly; we warm ourfelves
fafely while we ftand near the fire; but
if we feek to outface the one or enter
into the other, we forthwith become
blind or burnt. (H. W.)

Wifeft Own God.

This is certain, that if we look into
the wifdom of all ages we fhall find
that there never was man of folid
underftanding or excellent judgment;
never any man whofe mind the art of
education hath not bended; whofe eyes

a foolish superstition hath not afterwards blinded; whose apprehensions are sober and by a pensive inspection advised, but that he hath found by an unresistible necessity one true God and everlasting Being, all for ever causing and all for ever sustaining. (*Ibid.*)

All-seeing, All-knowing God.

But it is neither of examples the most lively instructions, nor the words of the wisest men, nor the terror of future torments, that hath yet so wrought in our blind and stupefied minds as to make us remember that the infinite eye and wisdom of God doth pierce through all our pretences; as to make us remember that the justice of God doth require none other accuser than our own consciences; which neither the false beauty of our apparent actions nor all the formality which (to pacify the opinions of men) we put on, can in any or the least kind, cover from His knowledge. And so much did that heathen wisdom confess, no way as yet qualified by the knowledge of a true

God. If any (faith Euripides), 'having in his life committed wickedneſs, think he can hide it from the everlaſting God, he thinks not well.' (*Ibid.*)

Heathen Gods Dead.

All theſe are vaniſhed. For the inventions of mortal men are no leſs mortal than themſelves. The Fire which the Chaldeans worſhipped for a god is crept into every man's chimney; which the lack of fuel ſtarveth, water quencheth, and want of air ſuffocateth. Jupiter is no more vexed with Juno's jealouſies. Death hath perſuaded him to chaſtity and her to patience. And that Time which hath devoured itſelf hath alſo eaten up both the bodies and images of him and her—yea, their ſtately temples of ſtone and dureful marble. The houſes and ſumptuous buildings erected to Baal can nowhere be found upon the earth, nor any monument of that glorious temple conſecrated to Diana. There are none now in Phenicia that lament the death

Sir Walter Raleigh.

of Adonis, nor any in Libya, Crete, Theffalia, or elfewhere that can afk counfel or help from Jupiter. The great god Pan hath broken his pipes. Apollo's priefts are become fpeechlefs; and the trade of riddles in oracles, with the Devil's telling men's fortunes therein, is taken up by counterfeit Egyptians [= gipfies] and cozening aftrologers. (H. W., B. i., c. vi.) ['Temple of Diana' redifcovered in our own time. See account of its magnificent ruins in Falkener (1862) and Guhl's 'Ephefiaca' (1843).]

GUIANA AND ITS COLONIZATION.

The Offer of Guiana to Queen Elizabeth Privately Affirmed, 1595.

To Sir Robert Cecil.

SIR,— You may perceive by this 'Relation' that it is no dream which I have reported of Guiana. And if one image [= idol ?] have been brought from thence weighing 47 kintalls [47 hundredweight], I know that in Manoa there are ſtore of theſe. If the 'Relation' ſent to the Spaniſh king had been alſo taken, you ſhould therein have found matter of great admiration [= wonder]. But however this action be reſpected, I know that the like fortune was never offered to any Chriſtian prince. I know it will be preſently followed both by the Spaniſh and French, and if it be foreſlowed by us I conclude that we are curſed of God. In the meantime that none be ſuffered to foil the enterpriſe, and that thoſe kings of the borders which are by my labour, peril and charge won to her Majeſty's love and obedience, be not by other pilferers loſt again; I hope I ſhall be thought worthy to direct thoſe actions that I have at mine own charges laboured in, and to govern that country which I have diſcovered and hope to conquer for the Queen without her coſt. I am ſending away a bark to the country to comfort and aſſure the people, that they deſpair not, nor yield to any compoſition with other nations.

I know the plot [= map of Guiana]

is by this time finished, which if you please command from Harriot, that her Majesty may see it. If it be thought of less importance than it deserveth, her Majesty will shortly bewail her negligence therein, and the enemy, by the addition of so much wealth, wear us out of all. Sir, I pray esteem it as the affair requireth if you love the Queen's honour, profit, and safety. If I be thought unworthy to be employed, or that because of my disgrace all men fear to adventure with me—if it may not be otherwise—I wish some other of better sufficiency and grace might undertake it, that the Queen lose not that which she shall never find again.

You find that there are besides gold, both diamonds and pearl . . . ('Letters,' pp. 109, 110.)

Expedition is preparing for 'Guiana,' 1595.
To Sir Robert Cecil.

For conclusion I will only say this much : take good heed lest you be not too flow. Expedition in a little is better than much too late. But you ministers of despatch are not plentiful. Neither is it every man's occupation. ('Letters,' pp. 108, 109.)

Another Appeal, 1595.

I beseech you let me know whether we shall be travellers or tinkers, conquerors or novices. For if the winter pass without making provision, there can be no victualling in the summer; and if it be now foreslowed, farewell Guiana for ever. Then must I determine to beg or run away. Honour and gold and all good for ever hopeless. ('Letters,' p. 117.)

The Falls of Caroli in Guiana, 1595.

Myself with Captain Gifford, Captain Caulfield, Edward Hancock, and some half a dozen shot, marched over land to view the strange overfalls of the river of Caroli, which roared so far off, and also to see the plains adjoining, and the rest of the province of Canuri. I sent also Captain Whiddon, W. Connock, and some eight shot with them, to see if they could find any mineral-stone along the river's side. When we ran to the tops of the first hills of the plains adjoining to the river, we beheld that wonderful breach of waters which ran down Caroli, and might from that mountain see the river how it ran in three parts above twenty miles off; and there appeared some ten or twelve overfalls in sight, every one as high over the other as a church tower, which fell with that fury that the rebound of waters made it seem as if it had been all covered over with a great shower of rain; and in some places we took it at the first for a smoke that had risen over some great town. For mine own part, I was well persuaded from thence to have returned, being a very ill footman, but the rest were all so desirous to go near the said strange thunder of waters, as they drew me on by little and little, till we came into the next valley, where we might better discern the same. I never saw a more beautiful country, nor more lovely prospects; hills so raised here and there over the valleys, the river winding into diverse branches, the plains adjoining without bush or stubble, all fair green grass, the ground of hard sand, easy to march on, either for horse or foot, the deer crossing in every path, the birds towards the evening singing on every tree with a thousand several tunes, cranes and herons of white, crimson, and carnation perching on the river's side, the air fresh with a gentle easterly wind, and every stone that we stooped to take up promised either gold or silver by his complexion. ('Discoverie.')

Wonders of Guiana noted by Shakespeare,
1595.

There is also another goodly river beyond Caroli, which is called Arui [=Aro], which also runneth through the lake Cassipa, and falleth into Orinoco farther west, making all the land between Caroli and Arui an island, which is likewise a most beautiful country. Next unto Arui [=Aro] there are two rivers,

Sir Walter Raleigh.

Atocca and Caora [= Caura], and on this branch, which is called Caora, are a nation of people whose heads appear not above their shoulders, which, though it may be thought a mere fable, yet for mine own part I am resolved it is true, because every child in the provinces of Aromara and Canuri affirms the same. They are called *Ewaipanoma*. They are reported to have their eyes in their shoulders and their mouths in the middle of their breasts, and that a long train of hair groweth backward between their shoulders. ('Discoverie.') [Shakespeare must have read Raleigh's 'Discovery of Guiana' [1595]. He makes use of this description of the Ewaipanoma when Othello gives Desdemona a relation of the wonders he had seen:

> 'The cannibals, that each other eat;
> The Anthropophagi, and men whose heads
> Do grow beneath their shoulders.'

Oldys says this reference was worked in as a compliment to Raleigh.]

Golden Dreams of Guiana, 1595-96.

If Peru had so many heaps of gold, whereof those *Ingas* [=Incas] were princes, and that they delighted so much therein, no doubt but this which now liveth and reigneth in *Manoa* hath the same humour, and I am assured hath more abundance of gold within his territory than all Peru and the West Indies. For the rest, which myself have seen, I will promise these things that follow and know to be true. Those that are desirous to discover and to see many nations, may be satisfied within this river, which bringeth forth so many arms and branches leading to several countries and proving above 2,000 miles east and west, and 800 miles south and north, and of these the most either rich in gold or in other merchandises. The common soldier shall here fight for gold and pay himself, instead of pence, with plates of half a foot broad, whereas he beareth his bones in other wars for poverty and penury. Those commanders and chieftains that shoot at honour and abundance, shall find there more rich and beautiful cities, more temples adorned with golden images, more sepulchres filled with treasure, than either Cortez found in Mexico, or Pizzarro in Peru, and the shining glory of this conquest will eclipse all these so far extended beams of the Spanish nation. ('Discoverie.')

The Pineapple.

Brought us . . . victuall, which they did in great plenty . . . with diverse sorts of excellent fruits and roots and great abundance of *Pinas*, the princess of fruits. ('Discoverie.')

Guiana Offered to Queen Elizabeth Publicly Affirmed, 1596.

The West Indies were first offered her Majesty's grandfather by Columbus, a stranger, in whom there might be doubt of deceit ; and besides, it was then thought incredible that there were such and so many lands and regions never written of before. This Empire is made known to her Majesty by her own vassal, and by him that oweth to her more duty than an ordinary subject; so that it shall ill sort with the many graces and benefits which I have received to abuse her highness either with fables or imaginations. The country is already discovered, many nations won to her Majesty's love and obedience; and those Spaniards which have latest and longest laboured about the conquest beaten out, discouraged, and disgraced, which among these nations were thought invincible. Her Majesty may, in this enterprise, employ all those soldiers and gentlemen that are younger brethren, and all captains and chieftains that want employment, and the charge will be only the first setting out in victualling and arming them; for after the first or second year I doubt not but to see in London a Contractation House of more receipt for Guiana than there is now in Seville for the West Indies.

And I am resolved that if there were but a small army afoot in Guiana, marching towards Manoa, the chief city of Inga, he would yield her Majesty by composition so many hundred thousand pounds yearly as should both defend all enemies abroad and defray all expenses at home, and that he would besides pay a garrison of 3,000 or 4,000 soldiers very royally to defend him against other nations; for he cannot but know how his predecessors—yea, how his own great-uncles, Guascar and Atibalipa, sons to Guanacapa, emperor of Peru—were (while they contended for the empire) beaten out by the Spaniards, and that both of late years, and ever since the said Conquest, the Spaniards have sought the passages and entry of his country; and of their cruelties used to the borderers he cannot be ignorant. In which respect no doubt but he will be brought to tribute with great gladness; if not, he hath neither shot nor iron weapon in all his empire, and therefore may easily be conquered.

And I further remember that Berreo confessed to me and others (which I protest before the majesty of God to be true) that there was found among prophecies in Peru (at such time as the empire was reduced to the Spanish obedience), in their chiefest temples, amongst divers others which foreshowed the loss of the said empire, that from Inglatierra those Ingas should be again in time to come restored and delivered from the servitude of the said conquerors. And I hope, as we note these few hands have displanted the first garrison, and driven them out of the said country, so her Majesty will give orders for the rest, and either defend it and hold it as tributary, or conquer and keep it as empress of the same; for whatsoever prince shall possess it shall be greatest; and if the king of Spain enjoy it, he shall become irresistible. Her Majesty hereby shall confirm and strengthen the opinions of all nations, as touching her great and princely actions. And where the South border of Guiana reacheth to the dominion and empire of the Amazones, there women shall hereby hear the name of a virgin which is not only able to defend her own territories and her neighbours', but also to invade and conquer so great empires and so far removed.

To speak more at this time, I fear, would be but troublesome. I trust in God, this being true, will suffice, and that He which is King of all kings and Lord of all lords will put it into her heart which is lady of ladies to possess it; if not, I will judge those men worthy to be kings thereof that, by her grace and leave, will undertake it of themselves. ('Discoverie of Guiana.')

Why More Gold was not Brought from Guiana, 1596.

For any longer stay to have brough a more quantity (which I hear hath been often objected), whosoever had seen or proved the fury of that river [Oronoque] after it began to arise, and had been a month and odd days, as we were, from hearing aught from our ships, leaving them meanly manned above 400 miles off, would perchance have turned somewhat sooner than we did, if all the mountains had been gold or rich stones, and to say the truth, all the branches and small rivers which fell into Oronoko were raised with such speed, as if we waded therein over the shoes in the morning outward, we were covered to the shoulders homeward the very same day, and to stay to dig out gold with our nails had been *opus laboris* but not *ingenii:* such a quantity as would have served our turns we could not have had but a discovery of the mines to our infinite disadvantage we had made, and that could have been the best profit of further search or stay; for those mines are not easily broken nor opened in haste, and I could have returned a good quantity of gold ready cast if I had not shot at another mark than present profit. ('Discoverie.')

Voyage to Guiana further pressed,
1615-16.

To Secretary Sir Ralph Winwoa.

HONOURED SIR,—I was lately persuaded by two gentlemen, my ancient friends, to acquaint your Honour with some offers of mine made heretofore for a journey to Guiana, who were of

Sir Walter Raleigh.

opinion that it would be better understood now than when it was first propounded; which advice having surmounted my despair, I have presumed to send unto your Honour the copies of those letters which I then wrote, both to his Majesty and to the Treasurer Cecil, wherein as well the reasons that first moved me are remembered, as the objections by him made are briefly answered.

What I know of the riches of that place, not by hearsay, but what mine eyes have seen, I have said it often, but it was then to no end: because those that had the greatest trust were resolved not to believe it; not because they doubted the truth, but because they doubted my disposition towards themselves, where [= in case that] (if God had blessed me in the enterprise) I had recovered his Majesty's favour and good opinion. Other cause than this or other suspicion, they never had any. Our late worthy Prince of Wales was extreme curious in searching out the nature of my offences; the Queen's Majesty has informed herself from the beginning; the King of Denmark at both times of his being here, was thoroughly satisfied of my innocence; they would otherwise never have moved his Majesty on my behalf.

The wife, the brother and the son of a king do not use to sue for men suspect; but, Sir, since they all have done it out of their charity, and but with reference to me alone, your Honour (whose respect hath only relation to his Majesty's service), strengthened by the example of those princes, may with the more hardness [= resolution] do the like, being princes to whom his Majesty's good estate is no less dear, and all men that shall oppugn it no less hateful than to the King himself.

It is true, Sir, that his Majesty hath sometimes answered that his Council knew me better than he did; meaning some two or three of them; and it was indeed my infelicity. For had his Majesty known me I had never been here where I now am; or had I known his Majesty, they had never been so long there where they now are. His Majesty not knowing of me hath been my ruin; and his Majesty misknowing of them hath been the ruin of a goodly part of his estate: but they are all of them now—some living and some dying—come to his Majesty's knowledge. But, Sir, how little soever his Majesty knew me, and how much soever he believed them, yet have I been bound to his Majesty both for my life and all that remains, of which but for his Majesty, no life or aught else had remained. In this respect, Sir, I am bound to yield up the same life and all that I have for his Majesty's service. To die for the King and not by the King is all the ambition I have in the world.—WALTER RALEGH. ('Letters,' pp. 339-341.)

Thanks for release from Tower,
1615-16, March 17.

To Sir George Villiers, afterwards Duke of Buckingham.

SIR,—You have by your mediation put me again into the world. I can but acknowledge it; for to pay any part of your favours by any return of mine as yet it is not in my power. If it fucceed well, a good part of the honours fhall be yours; and if I do not alfo make it profitable unto you, I fhall fhow myfelf exceeding ungrateful.

In the meanwhile, and until God difcover the fuccefs, I befeech you to reckon me among the number of your faithful fervants, though the leaft able. —W. RALEGH. ('Letters,' p. 341: fee alfo Raleigh's pathetic letter to Buckingham, pp. 373-375, of 1618.)

Legality of the Guiana Expedition of 1618.

To George Lord Carew of Clopton.

Becaufe I know not whether I fhall live to come before the Lords, I have for his Majefty's fatisfaction here fet down as much as I can fay, either for mine own defence or againft myfelf, as things are conftrued.

It is true that though I acquainted his Majefty with my intent to land in Guiana, yet I never made it known to his Majesty that the Spaniards had any footing there, neither had I any authority by my patent to remove the Spaniards from thence; and therefore his Majesty had no interest in the attempt of St. Thomas by any foreknowledge thereof in his Majesty.

But knowing his Majesty's title to the country to be the best and most Christian, because the natural lords did most willingly acknowledge Queen Elizabeth to be their sovereign, who by me promised to defend them from the Spanish cruelty, I made no doubt but that I might enter the land by force—seeing the Spaniards had no other title but force (the Pope's donation excepted); considering also that they got a possession divers years since my possession, taken for the Crown of England. For were not Guiana his Majesty's, then might I as well have been questioned for a thief for taking of gold out of the King of Spain's mines, as the Spaniards do now call me a peace-breaker: for from any territory confessed to be the King of Spain's it is no more lawful to take gold than lawful for the Spaniards to take tin out of Cornwall.

Now, were this poffeffion of theirs a fufficient bar to his Majefty's right, the Kings of Spain might as well call themfelves Dukes of Brittany becaufe they held Bluette and fortified there; and Kings of Ireland becaufe they poffeffed Smerwick and fortified there; and fo in other places.

That his Majefty was well refolved of his right there, I make no kind of doubt, becaufe the Englifh, both under Mr. Charles Leigh and Mr. Harcourt, had leave to plant and inhabit the country.

That Oronoque itfelf had [had] long ere this 5,000 Englifh in it, I affure myfelf—had not my employment at Cales [Cadiz] the next year after my return from Guiana, and after that our journey to the Iflands, hindered me for thefe two years; after which Tyrone's Rebellion made her Majefty unwilling that any great number of fhips or men fhould be taken out of England till that Rebellion were ended. And, laftly, her Majefty's death and my long imprifonment gave time to the Spaniards to fet up a town of ftakes covered with leaves of trees, upon the banks of the Oronoque, which they called St. Thomas; but they have neither reconciled nor conquered any of the Caſiques or natural lords of the country; which Caſiques are ſtill in arms againſt them, as by the Governor's letter to the King of Spain may appear.

That by landing in Guiana there can be any breach of peace, I think yet, under favour, impoſſible. To break peace where there is no peace, it cannot be.

That the Spaniards give us no peace there, it doth appear by the King's letter to his Governor, that they ſhall put to death all thoſe Spaniards and Indians that trade—*con los Engleſes enemigos*—with Engliſh enemies. Yea, thoſe very Spaniards which we encountered at St. Thomas did of late years murder 36 of Mr. Hall's men, of London, and mine, who landed, without weapons, upon the Spaniſh faith, to trade with them.* Mr. Thorne, alſo

---

* From 'Apology': 'If we had any peace with the Spaniards in those parts of the world, why did even those Spaniards which were now encountered, tie the six-and-thirty Englishmen out of Master Hall's ship of London and mine, back to back, and cut their throats after they had traded with them a whole month, and came to them ashore having not so much as a sword or any other weapon among them all?'

of Tower Street, in London, besides many other English, was in like sort murdered, the year before my delivery out of the Tower.

Now if this kind of trade be 'peaceable,' there is then a peaceable trade in the Indies between us and the Spaniards. But if this be cruel war and hatred and no peace, then there is no peace broken by our attempt. Again, how doth it stand with the greatness of the King of Spain first to call us 'enemies' when he did hope to cut us in pieces, and then, having failed, to call us peacebreakers; for to be an enemy and a peacebreaker in one and the same action is impossible. But the King of Spain, in his letter to the Governor of Guiana, dated at Madrill [Madrid], the 29th of March—before we left the Thames —calls us *Englefes enemigos*.

Had it pleased the King of Spain to have written to his Majesty in six months' time (for we were so long in preparing), and have made his Majesty know that our landing in Guiana would draw after it a breach of peace, I presume to think his Majesty would have stayed our enterprise for the present. This he might have done with less charges than to levy 300 soldiers and transport 10 pieces of ordnance from Puerto Rico; which soldiers, added to the garrison of St. Thomas (had they arrived before our coming), had overthrown all our said companies. And there would have followed no complaint.

For the vain point of landing near St. Thomas, it is true that we were of opinion that we must have driven the Spaniards out of this town before we could pass the thick woods upon the mountain of the mine, which, I confess, I did first resolve upon. But better bethinking myself, I referred the taking of the town to the goodness of the mine, which if they found to be so rich as it might persuade the leaving of a garrison there, then to drive the Spaniards thence. But to have it burnt was never my intent; neither could they give me any reason why they did it.

Upon the return, I examined the Sergeant-Major and Kemish why they followed not my last directions for the trial of the mine before the taking of the town. And they answered me that, although they durst hardly go to the mine, leaving a garrison of Spaniards behind them and their boats, yet they said they followed those later directions, and did land between the town and the mine; and that the Spaniards, without any manner of parley, set upon them unawares and charged them, calling them *Peros Engleses*, and by skirmishing with them drew them on to the very entrance of the town before they knew where they were; so as if any peace had been in those parts, the Spaniards first brake the peace and made the first slaughter. For as the English could not but land to seek the mine, being come thither to that end, so being first reviled and charged by the Spaniards, they could do no less than repel force by force.

Lastly, it is a matter of no small consequence to acknowledge we have offended the King of Spain by landing in Guiana. For, first, it weakens his Majesty's title to the country, or quits it; secondly, there is no king that hath ever given the least way to any other king or state in the traffic of the lives and goods of his subjects—to wit, as in our case, that it shall be lawful for the

Spaniards to murder us either by war or terror, and not lawful for us to defend ourselves and pay them with their own coin. . . . [MS. burned away here] . . . A French gentleman called Florie went thence with purpose and with commission to burn and to sack all places in the Indies that he could master; and yet hath the French King married a daughter of Spain.

 This is all that I can say, other than I have spent my poor estate, lost my son and my health, and endured as many sorts of miseries as ever man did, in hope to do his Majesty service; and have not, to my understanding, committed any hostile act other than the entrance upon a territory belonging to the crown of England, where the English were first set upon and slain by the usurping Spaniards.

 I invaded no other parts of the Indies pretended by the Spaniards. I returned unto England with the manifest peril of my life, with a purpose not to hold my life by any other act than his Majesty's grace, and from which no man nor any peril could dissuade me. To that grace, and goodness, and kingliness

I refer myself; which, if it shall find that I have not yet suffered enough, it may, if it please, add more affliction to the remainder of a wretched life. [Also burned away.] ('Letters,' pp. 375-380. Cf. 'Apology' for brief account of the facts.)

On the Death of Walter Raleigh, in Guiana, March 22, 1618.

To Lady Raleigh.

I was loath to write, because I knew not how to comfort you; and God knows I never knew what sorrow meant till now. All that I can say to you is, that you must obey the will and providence of God, and remember that the Queen's Majesty bare the loss of the Prince Henry with a magnanimous heart, and the Lady Harrington of her only son. Comfort your heart (dearest Bess); I shall sorrow for us both. I shall sorrow the less because I have not long to sorrow, because not long to live. I refer you to Mr. Secretary

Winwood's letter, who will give you a copy of it if you send for it. Therein you shall know what hath passed. I have written but that letter, for my brains are broken, and it is a torment for me to write, and especially of misery. I have desired Mr. Secretary to give my Lord Carew a copy of his letter. I have cleansed my ship of sick men, and sent them home. I hope God will send us somewhat ere we return. Commend me to all at Lothbury. You shall hear from me, if I live, from the Newfoundland, where I mean to make clean my ship and revictual, for I have tobacco enough to pay for it. The Lord bless and comfort you, that you may bear patiently the death of your valiant son. Yours, W. RALEGH.

22nd of March [1618], from the Isle of Christopher.

[Postcript.]—I protest before the majesty of God that, as Sir Francis Drake and Sir John Hawkins died heart-broken when they failed of their enterprise, I could willingly do the like, did I not contend against sorrow for your sake, in hope to provide somewhat

for you and to comfort and relieve you.
If I live to return, refolve yourfelf
that it is the care for you that hath
ftrengthened my heart. It is true that
Kemifh might have gone directly to
the mine, and meant it. But, after
my fon's death, he made them to believe
he knew not the way, and excufed himfelf upon the want of water in the
river, and, counterfeiting many impedi-
ments, left it unfound. When he came
back I told him that he had undone me,
and that my credit was loft for ever.

He anfwered that when my fon was
loft, and that he left me fo weak that
he refolved not to find me alive, he
had no reafon to enrich a company of
rafcals, who, after my fon's death, made
no accompt of him. He further told
me that the Englifh fent up into
Guiana could hardly defend the Spanifh
town of St. Thomas, which they had
taken, and therefore for them to pafs
through thick woods, it was impoffible;
and more impoffible to have victuals
brought them into the mountain. And
it is true that the governor Diego
Polemeque and four other captains,
being flain, of which my fon Watte

[= Walter] slew one; Pleffington, Watt's servant, and John of Moroccoes, one of his men, slew other two. I say, five of them being slain in the entrance of the town, the rest went off in a whole body and took more care to defend the passage to their mines (of which they had three within a league of the town, besides a mine that was about 5 miles off) than they did of the town itself. Yet Kemish at the first was resolved to go to the mine; but when he came to the bankside to the land, he had two of his men slain outright from the bank and six others hurt, and Captain Thornix shot in the head, of which wound and the accidents thereof he hath pined away these twelve weeks.

Now when Kemish came back and gave me the four reasons which moved him not to open the mine—the one, the death of my son; the second, the weakness of the English and their impossibilities to work and to be victualled; a third, that it was a folly to discover it for the Spaniards; and the last, both my weakness and my being unpardoned —and that I rejected all these arguments, and told him that I must leave it to himself to answer it to the King and the State, he shut up himself into his cabin and shot himself with a pocket-pistol, which brake one of his ribs; and, finding it had not prevailed, he thrust a long knife under his other ribs up to the handle, and died. Thus much I have writ to Mr. Secretary, to whose letters I refer you. But, because I think my friends will rather hearken after you than any other to know the truth, I did, after the sailing back, open your letter again, to let you know in brief the state of that business; which I pray you impart to my Lord of Northumberland, and Silvanus Scory and to Sir John Leigh.

For the rest, there was never poor man so exposed to the slaughter as I was; for being commanded upon my allegiance to set down, not only the country, but the very rivers, by which I was to enter it—to name my ships, number my men and my artillery; this was sent by the Spanish Ambassador forthwith to the King of Spain. The King wrote his letters to all parts of the Indies, especially to the gentlemen of consequence of Guiana, El Dorado and Trinidado; of which the first letter bore date the 19th of March, 1617, at Madrill [= Madrid], when I had not yet left the Thames: which letter I have sent Mr. Secretary. I have also two other letters of the King's which I reserve, and one of the Council. The King also sent a commission to levy 300 soldiers out of his garrisons of Nuevo Reigno de Granadoes and Porto Rico, with ten pieces of brass ordnance to entertain us. He also prepared an armada by sea to set upon us. It were too long to tell you how we were pressed. If I live I shall make it known. My brains are broken, and I cannot write much. I live yet, and I have told you why. Whitney, for whom I sold my plate at Plymouth, and to whom I gave more credit and countenance than all the captains of my fleet, ran from me at the Granadoes, and Woolaston with him; so as I own now but five ships, and one of these I have sent home—my fly-boat—and in her a rabble of idle rascals, which I know will not spare to wound me; but I care not. I am sure there is never a base slave in the fleet hath taken the pains and care that I have done; hath flept so little and travailed so much. My friends will not believe them; and for the rest I care not. God in heaven bless and strengthen your heart. Yours, W. RALEGH. ('Letters,' pp. 359-363. See under 'Guiana.')

HONOUR.

If we hold it no difgrace to submit ourselves for the recovery of our debts, goods, and lands, and for all things else by which the lives of ourselves, our wives and children are fuftained, to the judges of the land, because it may be felony to take by violence even that which is our own, why fhould we not fubmit ourselves to the judges of honour in cafes of honour, becaufe to recover our reputation by ftrong hand may be murder? But yet, again, it may be objected that the lofs of honour ought to be more fearful unto us than either the lofs of our goods, of our lands, or of our lives; and I fay fo too. But what is this honour—I mean honour indeed—

and that which ought to be so dear unto us, other than a kind of history or fame, following actions of virtue, actions accompanied with difficulty or danger, and undertaken for the public good? In these, he that is employed and trusted, if he fail in the performance either through cowardice or any other base affection, it is true that he loseth his honour. But the acting of a private combat for a private respect, and most commonly a frivolous one, is not an action of virtue, because it is contrary to the law of God and of all Christian kings; neither is it difficult, because even and equal in persons and arms; neither for a public good, but tending to the contrary, because the loss or mutilation of an able man is also a loss to the commonweal. (H. W., B. v., c. iii.)

INJUSTICE.

Certainly, with more patience men are wont to endure the loss that befell them by mere casualty than the damage they sustain by means of injustice, because these are accompanied with sense of indignity, whereof the other are free. When robbers break into men's homes and spoil them, they tell the owners plainly that money they want, and money they must have. But when a judge, corrupted by reward, hatred, favours, or any other passion, takes both home and land from the rightful owner and bestows them upon some friend of his own or his favourite, he says that the rule of justice will have it so; that it is the voice of the law and ordinance of God Himself: and what else harm doth he, than by a kind of circumlocution tell his humble suppliants that he holds them idiots or base wretches, not able to get relief? Must it not astonish and, withal, vex any man of a free spirit when he sees none other difference between the judge and the thief than in the manner of performing of their exploits: as if the whole being of justice consisted in point of formality? In such case, an honest subject will either seek remedy by ordinary courses, or wait his time till God shall place better men in office, and call the oppressors to account. But a stranger will not do so; he hath nothing to do with the affairs of Barbary, neither concerns it him what officers be placed or difplaced in Tarradanto, or whether Mulifidian himfelf can contain the kingdom: his fhop and goods are unjuftly taken from him, and, therefore, he will feek leave to right himfelf if he can, and return the injury tenfold upon the whole nation from which he received it. Truth is, that men are fooner weary to dance attendance at the gates of foreign lords than to tarry the good leifure of their own magiftrates; nor do they bear fo quietly the lofs of fome parcel confifcate abroad as the greater detriment which they fuffer by fome prowling vice-admiral, cuftomer, or public minifter at their return. ('Difcoverie.')

INSTINCT.

The law of nature in general I take to be that difpofition, inftinct, and formal quality which God in His eternal providence hath given and imprinted in the nature of every creature, animate and inanimate. And as it is *divinum lumen* in man, enlightening our formal reason, so is it more than sense in beasts and more than vegetation in plants. For it is not sense alone in beasts which teacheth them at first sight and without experience or instruction to fly from the enemies of their lives; seeing that bulls and horses appear unto the sense more fearful and terrible than the least kind of dogs, and yet the hare and deer feed by the one and fly from the other—yea, though by them never seen before, and that as soon as they fell from their dams. Neither is it sense which hath taught other beasts to provide for winter: birds to build their nests high or low, according to the tempestuous or quiet seasons; or the birds of India to make their nests on the smallest twigs which hang over rivers and not on any other part of the tree or elsewhere, to save their eggs and young ones from the monkeys and other beasts, whose weight such a twig could not bear, and which would fear to fall into the water. The instances in this kind are exceeding many which may be given. Neither is it out of the vegetable or growing nature of plants, that some trees, as the female of the palmetto, will not bear any fruit except the male grow in sight. But this they do by that law which the infinite and unsearchable wisdom of God had in all eternity provided for them and for every nature created. (H. W., B. ii., c. iii.)

KINGS AND KINGDOMS.

Kings—in what Sort exempt from Human Laws.

Whether the power of the human law be without exception of any person, it is doubtfully disputed among those that have written of this subject, as well divines as lawyers; and namely, Whether sovereign princes be compellable, yea or no? But whereas there are two powers of the law, as aforesaid, the one directive, the other coactive, to the power directive they ought to be subject, but not to that which constraineth. For as touching violence or punishments, no man is bound to give a prejudicial judgment against himself; and if equals have not any power over each other, much less have inferiors over their superiors, from whom they receive their authority and strength. And speaking of the supreme power of laws, simply then is the prince so much above the laws as the soul and body united is above a dead and senseless carcase. For the king is truly called *jus vivum et lex animata*, 'an animate and living law.' But this is true, that by giving authority to laws, princes both add greatness to themselves and conserve it, and therefore was it said of Bracton, out of Justinian: 'Rightfully ought the king to attribute that to the law which the law first attributeth to the king, for it is the law that doth make kings.' But whereas Bracton (p. 2) ascribeth this power to the human law, he is therein mistaken. For kings are made by God, and laws divine, and by human laws only declared to be kings. As for the places remembered by the divines and lawyers which infer a kind of obligation of princes, they teach no other thing therein than the law of conscience and profit arising from the examples of virtuous princes, who are to give an account of their actions to God only. (H. W., B. ii., c. iv.)

BRAVE AND NOBLE WORDS TO THE KING OF ENGLAND (JAMES I.).

Most Gracious Sovereign,—Those that are suppressed and helpless are commonly silent, wishing that the common ill in all sort might be with their particular misfortunes; which disposition, as it is uncharitable in all men, so it would be in me more dog-like than man-like to bite the stone that struck me—to wit, the borrowed authority of my sovereign misinformed, seeing that arms and hands that flung it are most of them already rotten. For I must confess it ever that they are debts and not discontentments that your Majesty hath laid upon me— the debts and obligations of a friendless adversity, far more payable in all kinds than those of the prosperous: all which, nor the least of them, though I cannot discharge, I may yet endeavour it. And, notwithstanding my restraint hath retrenched all ways, as well the ways of labour and work, as of all other employments, yet hath it left with me my cogitations, than which I have nothing else to offer on the altar of my love.

Of these (most gracious Sovereign) I have used some part in the following dispute between a Counsellor of State and a Justice of the Peace, the one dissuading, the other persuading, the calling of Parliament. In all which, since the Norman Conquest (at the least, so many as histories have gathered) I have in some things in the following dispute presented your Majesty with the contents and successes.

Some things there are, and those of the greatest, which because they ought to be resolved on, I thought fit to range them in the front of the rest, to the end your Majesty may be pleased to examine your own great and princely heart of their acceptance or refusal.

The first is, that supposition that your Majesty's subjects give nothing but with adjunction of their own interest, interlacing in one and the same act your Majesty's relief and their own liberties; not that your Majesty's piety was ever suspected, but because the best princes are ever the least jealous, your Majesty judging others by yourself who have abused your

Majesty's trust. The feared continuance of the like abuse may persuade the provision. But this caution, however it seemeth at first sight, your Majesty shall perceive by many examples following, but frivolous. The bonds of subjects to their kings should always be wrought out of iron, the bonds of kings unto subjects but with cobwebs.

Thus it is (most renowned Sovereign) that this traffic of assurances hath been often urged, of which if the conditions have been easy, our kings have as easily kept them; if hard and prejudicial, either to their honour or estates, the creditors have been paid their debt with their own presumption.

For all binding of a king by law upon the advantage of his necessity makes the breach itself lawful in a king, his charters and all other instruments being no other than the surviving witnesses of unconstrained will: *Princeps non subjicitur nisi, sua voluntate libera, mero rictu et certa scientia:* necessary words in all the grants of a king, in showing that the same grants were given freely and knowingly.

The second resolution will rest in your Majesty leaving the new impofitions, all monopolies, and other grievances of the people to the confideration of the Houfe [of Commons], provided that your Majefty's revenue be not abated; which, if your Majefty fhall refufe, it is thought that the difputes will laft long and the iffues will be doubtful; and, on the contrary, if your Majefty vouchfafe it, it may perchance be ftyled a yielding, which feemeth by the found to brave the regality. But (moft excellent Prince) what other is it to the ears of the wife but as the found a trumpet, having blafted forth a falfe alarm, becomes the common air? Shall the head yield to the feet? Certainly it ought, when they are grieved; for wifdom will rather regard the commodity than object the difgrace; feeing if the feet be in fetters the head cannot be fed, and where the feet feel but their own pains the head doth not only fuffer by participation, but withal by confideration of the evil.

Certainly the point of honour well weighed, hath nothing in it to even the balance; for, by your Majefty's favour, your Majefty doth not yield either to any perfon or to any power, but to difpute only, in which the propofition and minor prove nothing without a conclufion; which no other perfon or power can make but a majefty: yea, this in Henry the Third's time was called a wifdom incomparable. For the king raifed again, recovered his authority: for being in that extremity that he was driven with the queen and his children *cum ablatibus et prioribus fatis humilibus hofpitia quærere et prandia.* For the reft, may it pleafe your Majefty to confider, that there can nothing befall your Majefty in matters of affairs more unfortunately, than meeting the Commons of Parliament with ill fuccefs: a difhonour fo perfuafive and adventurous as it will not only find arguments, but it will take the leading of all enemies that fhall offer themfelves againft your Majefty's eftate.

Le tabourin de la pauvreté ne fait point de bruit: of which dangerous difeafe in princes the remedy doth chiefly confift in the love of the people; which how it may be had and held, no man knows better than your Majefty; how to lofe it all men know, and know that it is loft by nothing more than by the defence of others in wrong doing: the only motives of mischances that ever came to kings of this land since the Conquest.

It is only love (most renowned Sovereign) must prepare the way for your Majesty's following desires. It is love which obeys, which suffers, which gives, which sticks at nothing; which love, as well of your Majesty's people as the love of God to your Majesty, that it may always hold, shall be the continual prayers of your Majesty's most humble vassal, WALTER RALEGH. (Epistle dedicatory of 'Prerogative of Parliaments.')

ADVICE TO KINGS.

Counsellor. . . . I would fain know the man that durst persuade the king to call a Parliament; for if it should succeed ill in what case were he? *Justice.* You say well for yourself, my Lord, and perchance you that are lovers of yourselves (under pardon) do follow the advice of the late Duke of Alva, who was ever opposite to all resolutions in business

of importance; for if the things enter-
prised succeeded well the advice never
came in question; if ill (whereto great
undertakings are commonly subject),
he then made his advantage by remembering his contrary counsel: but, my
good Lord, these reserved politicians are
not the best servants; for he that is
bound to adventure his life for his
master is also bound to adventure his
advice: 'Keep not back counsel,' saith
Ecclesiasticus, 'when it may do good.'
(' Prerogative of Parliaments.')

AMBITION.

The power of ambition which possesseth the minds of men is such as rarely
or never sufficeth them to rest: the
reason thereof is that Nature hath
framed in them a certain disposition to
desire all things but not power to obtain
them; so as our desires being greater
than our power, thereof followeth discontent and evil satisfaction. Hereof
also proceedeth the variation of fortune; for some men desiring to get and

others fearing to lose that they have gotten, do occasion one man to injure another, and consequently public wars do follow; by means whereof one country is ruined and another enlarged. (Cab.)

NOBILITY AND FAVOURITES.

By keeping that degree and due proportion that neither they exceed in number more than the realm or State can bear, as the Scottish kingdom, and sometimes the English, when the realm was overcharged with the number of dukes, earls, and other nobles; whereby the authority of the prince was eclipsed and the realm troubled with their factions and ambitions. . . . Nor must it be neglected that not 'anyone so excel in honour, power, or wealth, as that he resembles another king within the kingdom' as the house of Lancaster within the realm. To that end, not to load any with too much honour and preferment, because it is hard even for the best and worthiest men to bear their greatness and high fortune temperately, as appeareth by infinite examples in all States. The sophisms [= wise maxims] for preventing or reforming this inconvenience are to be used with great caution and wisdom. If any great person be to be abated, not to deal with him by calumniation or forged matter, and so to cut him off without desert; especially if he be gracious among the people; which, besides the injustice, is an occasion many times of great danger towards the prince. Nor to withdraw their honour all at once, which maketh a desperate discontentment in the party, and a commiseration in the people, and so begetteth greater love towards him if he be already gracious for his virtue and public service. Nor to banish him into foreign countries, where he may have opportunity of practising [= plotting] with foreign States; whereof great danger may ensue, as in the example of Coriolanus, Henry IV., and such like. But to use these and the like sophisms, viz., to abate their greatness by degrees, as David, Joab, Justinian, Belisarius, etc.; to advance some other men to as great or greater honour, to shadow or over-mate the greatness of the other; to draw from him by degrees his friends and followers, by preferments, rewards, and other good and lawful means; especially, to be provided that these great men be not employed in great and powerful affairs of the Commonwealth, whereby they may have more opportunity to sway the State. (M.)

Enlarging Dominions.

He that enlargeth his dominions doth not always increase his power; but he that increaseth in force as well as in dominion, shall thereby grow great; otherwise he gaineth no more than is shortly to be lost, and consequently he ruineth himself; for he who spends more on the war than he gains by victory, loseth both labour and cost. (Cab.)

Ancient Kingdoms vanished.

Who hath not observed what labour, practice [= conspiracy], feud, bloodshed, and cruelty the kings and princes of the world have undergone, exercifed, taken on them and committed, to make themfelves and their iffues mafters of the world? And yet hath Babylon, Perfia, Egypt, Syria, Macedon, Carthage, Rome, and the reft, no fruit, flower, grafs, nor leaf, fpringing upon the face of the earth of thofe feeds. No, their very roots and ruins do hardly remain. (Cab.)

King near his Ruin.

A prince fheweth his ruin at hand whenfoever he beginneth to break the laws and cuftoms which are ancient and have been long time obeyed by the people of his dominion. (Cab.)

Royal Favourites.

That prince which careth to keep himfelf fecure from confpiracy ought rather to fear thofe to whom he hath done over-great favours than them whom he hath much injured; for thefe want opportunities, the other do not; and both their desires are as one, because the appetite of commanding is always as much or more than the desire of revenge. (Cab.)

Commonwealth.

A Commonwealth is the swerving or depravation of a free or popular State, or the government of the whole multitude of the base and poorer sort, without respect of the other orders. These two States, to wit, the Oligarchy and Commonwealth, are very adverse the one to the other, and have many bickerings between them. For that the richer or nobler sort suppose a right or superiority to appertain unto them in every respect, because they are superior but in some respects only, to wit, in riches, birth, parentage, etc. On the other side, the common people suppose there ought to be an equality in all other things, and in some State matters, because they are equal with the rich or noble, touching their liberty; whereas, indeed, neither the one nor the other are simply equal or superior, as touching government and fitness thereunto, because they are such, to wit, because they are rich, noble, free, etc., but because they are wise, virtuous, valiant, etc., and so have fit parts to govern a State. The several States are sometimes mixed and interwrought one with the other, yet even so as that the one hath eminence or predomination over the other, as in the humours and complexions of the body. So in the Roman State, the people had their *plebiscita*, and gave the suffrage in the election of magistrates, yet the Senate (as the State stood) for the most part swayed the State and bore the chief rule. So in the Venetian State, the Duke seemeth to represent a monarch, and the Senate to be his council; yet the Duke hath no power in State matters, but is like a head set on by art that beareth no brain. And so that State is senatorical and aristocratical. (M.)

RULES AND AXIOMS FOR PRESERVING OF A KINGDOM, HEREDITARY OR CONQUERED.

Prerogative.

By the tempering and moderation of the princely power and prerogative. For the less and more temperate their power and state is, the more firm and stable is their kingdom and government; because they seem to be farther off from a master-like and tyrannical empire, and less unequal in condition to the next degree, to wit, the nobility, and so less subject to grudge and envy. (M.)

Free or Popular State.

The popular state is the government of a State by the choicest sort of people, tending to the public good of all sort, viz., with due respect of the better, nobler and richer sort. In every just State some part of the government is, or ought to be, imparted to the people: as in a kingdom, a voice or suffrage in making laws; and sometimes also in levying of arms (if the charge be great and the Prince forced to borrow help of his subjects) the matter rightly may be propounded to a Parliament, that the tax may seem to have proceeded from themselves. So consultations and proceedings in judicial matters may in part be referred to them. The reason, lest seeing themselves to be in no number nor of reckoning, they mislike the State or kind of government: and where the multitude is discontented there must needs be many enemies to the present State. For which cause tyrants (which allow the people no manner of dealing in State matters) are forced to bereave them of their wealth and weapons, and all other means whereby they may resist or amend themselves, as in Rushland [= Russia], Turkey, etc. (M.)

Administration of Justice.

The good and direct administration of justice is in all places a principal part of government; for seldom or never shall we see any people discontented and desirous of alteration where justice is equally administered without respect of persons; and in every State this condition is required, but most of all in countries that do front upon other princes or were lately conquered. Hereunto the Prince's vigilancy and the magistrates' uprightness are especially required; for oftentimes the prince is deceived and the magistrates corrupted. It behoveth also the prince to maintain the judges and ministers of justice in their reputation, and yet to have a vigilant eye upon their proceedings, and the rather if their authority do include equity, and from their censure [=judgment] be no appeal; and if their office be during life, and they are men born and dwelling in the same country; all these things are to be duly considered of the prince: for as to call the judges into question is as it were to disgrace the judicial seat, so to wink at their corruptions were matter of just discontent to the subject. In this case, therefore, the prince cannot do more than by his wisdom to make choice of good men, and being chosen, to hold them in good reputation, so as the ordinary course of justice may proceed ; for otherwise great disorder, contempt and general confusion will ensue thereof. Secondly, he is to keep his eye upon their proceedings ; and lastly, to reserve unto himself a supreme power of appellation. (Cab.)

Royal Example.

Subjects are made good by two means, viz., by constraint of law and the prince's example ; for in all estates the people do imitate those conditions whereunto they see the prince inclined. Cf. Quintillian. (Cab.)

Punishments.

Punishments, impositions and censure are in all States necessary, although they shew and seem terrible, and consequently breed a certain desperation in subjects unless they be discreetly and modestly used; for extreme and frequent punishments taste of cruelty; great and many imposts favour of covetousness; censure of manners, when it exceedeth the quality of offences, doth seem rigorous in these matters; therefore it behoveth the prince to be moderate and cautelous [= cautious], chiefly in capital punishment, which must be confined within the bounds of justice: *Sit apud principem parsimonia etiam vilissimi sanguinis.* Seneca. (Cab.)

Dissimulation.

Dissimulation is as it were begotten by diffidence, a quality in princes of so great necessity as moved the Emperor Tiberius to say, *Nescit regnare qui nescit dissimulare.* The necessity of dissimulation is chiefly to be used with strangers and enemies. It also sheweth a certain discretion in magistrates sometimes to disguise with friends when no offence doth thereof follow: *Doli non doli sunt, nisi astu colas.* Plautus. This kind of craft, albeit in every man's conceit not praiseable, is nevertheless tolerable; and for princes and magistrates (the same being used to good ends) very necessary. But those cunnings which are contrary to virtue ought not of honest men to be used; neither dare I commend adulation and corruption, though they be often used in Court and are of some learned writers allowed: *Decipere pro moribus temporum, prudentia est.* Plautus. (Cab.)

Heroical Virtue in Kings.

To be a good Governor is a rare commendation, and to prefer the weal public above all respects whatsoever, is the virtue justly termed heroical. Of this virtue many ages afford not many examples. Hector is named by Aristotle as one of them, and defervedly if this praife be due to extraordinary height of fortitude ufed in defence of a man's own country. But if we confider that a love of the general good cannot be perfect without reference unto the Fountain of all goodnefs; we fhall find that no moral virtue how great foever can by itfelf deferve the commendation of more than virtue, as the *heroical* doth. Wherefore we muft fearch the Scriptures for patterns hereof; fuch as David, Jehofhaphat and Jofiah were, of Chriftian kings. If there were many fuch the world would foon be happy. It is not my purpofe to wrong the work of any, by denying the praife where it is due or by preferring a lefs excellent. But he that can find a king religious and zealous in God's caufe, without enforcement either of adverfity or of fome regard of State; a procurer of the general peace and quiet; who not only ufeth his authority but adds the travail of his eloquence in admonifhing his judges to do juftice; by the vigorous influence of whofe government civility is infufed even into thofe places that had been the dens of favage robbers and cut-throats; one that hath quite abolished a slavish Brehon law, by which a whole nation of his subjects were held in bondage [=Ireland], and one whose higher virtue and wisdom doth make the praise not only of nobility and other ornaments, but of abstinence from the blood, the wives and the goods of those that are under his power, together with a world of chief commendations belonging unto some good princes to appear less regardable: he, I say, that can find such a king, findeth an example worthy to add unto virtue an honourable title, if it were formerly wanting. Under such a king it is likely by God's blessing that a land shall flourish, with increase of trade, in countries before unknown, that civility and religion shall be propagated into barbarous and heathen countries, and that the happiness of his subjects shall cause the nations far off removed to wish him their sovereign. (M.)

LAW.

Authority above Law.

A wise man ought not to desire to inhabit that country where men have more authority than laws. (Cab.)

Magna Charta.

My good Lord, if you will give me leave to speak freely, I say that they are not well advised that persuade the king not to admit the *Magna Charta* with the former reservations; for as the king can never lose a farthing by it . . . so except England were as Naples is, and kept by garrisons of another nation, it is impossible for a King of England to greaten and enrich himself by any way so assuredly as by the love of his people; for by one rebellion the king hath more loss than by a hundred years' observance of *Magna Charta*. For therein have our kings been forced to compound with rogues and rebels, and to pardon them; yea, the state of the king, the monarchy, the nobility, have been endangered by them. (Prerogative of Parliaments.)

Parliament.

The Kings of England have never received lofs by Parliament; or prejudice. (Prerogative of Parliaments.)

Power.

It is an old country proverb that Might overcomes Right: a weak title that wears a ftrong fword commonly prevails againft a ftrong title that wears but a weak one. (Prerogative of Parliaments.)

Loyalty.

I fay the people are as loving to their king now as ever they were if they be honeftly and wifely dealt withal; and fo his Majefty had found them in his laft two Parliaments, if he had not been betrayed by thofe whom he moft trufted. (Prerogative of Parliaments.)

Queen Elizabeth Accessible.

Queen Elizabeth would set the reason of a mean man before the authority of the greatest counsellor she had; and by her patience therein she raised, upon the usual and ordinary customs of London, without any new imposition, above £50,000 a year. For though the treasurer Burleigh, and the Earl of Leicester and Secretary Walsingham, all three pensioners to customer Smith, did set themselves against a poor waiter of the custom-house, called Carwarden, and commanded the grooms of the privy-chamber not to give him access; yet the Queen sent for him and gave him countenance against them all. It would not serve the turn with her when your lordships would tell her that the disgracing her great officers by hearing the complaints of busy heads was a dishonour to herself; but she had always the answer: 'That if any man complain unjustly against a magistrate, it was reason that he should be severely punished; if justly, she was the Queen of the small as well as of the great, and would hear their complaints.' For a prince that suffereth himself to be besieged [=shut up, inaccessible] forsaketh one of the greatest regalities belonging to a monarchy, to wit, the last appeal, or, as the French call it, *le dernier reſſort*. (Prerogative of Parliaments.)

LIFE AND DEATH.

'The Port of Death.'

Let every man value his own wisdom as he pleaseth: let the rich man think all fools, that cannot equal his abundance; the revenger esteem all negligent that have not trodden down their opposites; the politician, all gross, that cannot merchandise their faith; yet, when we once come in sight of the port of Death, to which all winds drive us, and when, by letting fall that fatal anchor which can never be weighed again, the navigation of this life takes end; then it is, I say, that our own cogitations (those sad and severe cogitations formerly beaten from us by our health and felicity) return again and pay us to the uttermoſt for all the pleaſing paſſages of our lives paſt. It is then that we cry out to God for mercy; then, when ourſelves can no longer exerciſe cruelty towards others: and it is only then that we are ſtrucken through the ſoul with this terrible ſentence, that 'God will not be mocked' (Galatians vi. 7). For if, according to St. Peter, 'the righteous ſcarcely be ſaved' (1 Peter iv. 18), and that 'God ſpared not His angels' (2 Peter ii. 4), where ſhall thoſe appear, who, having ſerved their appetites all their lives, preſume to think that the ſevere commandments of the all-powerful God were given but in ſport; and that the ſhort breath which we draw when Death preſſeth us, if we can but faſhion it to the ſound of mercy (without any kind of ſatisfaction or amends), is ſufficient. 'O *quam multi*,' ſaith a reverend father, '*cum hac ſpe ad æternos labores et bella deſcendunt*.' (Preface, H. W.)

Death of the Righteous—Real and Spurious.

I confess that it is a great comfort to our friends, to have it said that we ended well; for we all desire (as Balaam did), to 'die the death of the righteous.' But what shall we call a disesteeming, an opposing, or, indeed, a mocking of God, if those men do not oppose Him, disesteem Him and mock Him, that think it enough for God to ask Him forgiveness at leisure, with the remainder and last drawing of a malicious breath? For what do they otherwise, that die this kind of well-dying, but say unto God as followeth: We beseech Thee, O God, that all the falsehoods, forswearing and teaching of our lives past, may be pleasing unto Thee; that Thou wilt for our sakes (that has had no leisure to do anything for Thine) change Thy nature (though impossible), and forget to be a just God; that Thou wilt love injuries and oppressions; call ambition wisdom and charity foolishness? For shall I prejudice my son (which I am resolved not to do), if I make restitution and confess myself to have been unjust (which I am too proud to do), if I deliver the oppressed? Certainly these wise worldlings have either found out a new God, or have made one; and in all likelihood such a leaden one as Louis the Eleventh wore in his cap; which, when he had caused any that he feared or hated to be killed, he would take it from his head and kiss it, beseeching it to pardon him this one evil act more and it should be the last; which (as at other times) he did, when by the practice [= plotting] of a Cardinal and a falsified sacrament, he caused the Earl of Armagnac to be stabbed to death; mockeries indeed fit to be used towards a leaden, but not towards the ever-living God. (*Ibid.*)

Fortunate and Wretched.

Now, for the rest, if we truly examine the difference of both conditions, to wit, of the rich and mighty, whom we call fortunate, and of the poor and oppressed, whom we account wretched; we shall find the happiness of the one and the miserable estate of the other, so tied by God to the very instant, and both so subject to interchange (witness the sudden downfall of the greatest princes and the speedy uprising of the meanest persons), as the one hath nothing so certain whereof to boast, nor the other so uncertain whereof to bewail itself. For there is no man so assured of his honour, of his riches, health or life, but that he may be deprived of either or all the very next hour or day to come. *Quid vesper vehat, incertum est:* 'What the evening will bring with it, it is uncertain' (James iv. 14); 'And yet ye cannot tell' (saith St. James) 'what shall be to-morrow. To-day he is set up, and to-morrow he shall not be found; for he is turned into dust, and his purpose perisheth.' And although the air which compasseth adversity be very obscure, yet therein we better discern God than in that shining light which environeth worldly glory; through which, for the clearness thereof, there is no vanity which escapeth our sight. And let adversity seem what it will; to happy men ridiculous, who make themselves merry at other men's misfortunes, and to those under the Cross, grievous; yet this is true, that for all that is past, to the very instant, the portions remaining are equal to either. For be it that we have lived many years, and (according to Solomon) 'in them all we have rejoiced'; or be it that we have measured the same length of days and therein have evermore sorrowed; yet, looking back from our present being, we find both the one and the other, to wit, the joy and the woe, failed out of sight, and Death, which doth pursue us and hold us in check from our infancy hath gathered it. *Quicquid ætatis retro est, mors tenet:* 'Whatsoever of our age is past, Death holds it.' (*Ibid.*)

Sorrows of this Life.

For myself, this is my consolation, and all that I can offer to others, that the sorrows of this life are but of two sorts: whereof the one hath respect to God, the other to the world. In the first, we complain to God against ourselves for our offences against Him, and confess: *Et tu justus es in omnibus quæ venerunt super nos,* 'And Thou, O Lord, art just in all that hath befallen us.' In the second, we complain to ourselves against God as if He had done us wrong, either in not giving us worldly goods and honours answering our appetites, or for taking them again from us having had them; forgetting that humble and just acknowledgment of Job, 'The Lord hath given and the Lord hath taken' (c. i., v. 21). To the first of which St. Paul hath promised blessedness, to the second death. And out of doubt he is either a fool or ungrateful to God, or both, that doth not acknowledge, how mean soever his estate be, that the same is yet far greater than that which God oweth him; or doth not acknowledge, how sharp soever his afflictions be, that the same are yet far less than those which are due unto him. And if an heathen wise man call the adversities of the world but *tributa vivendi,* 'the tributes of living,' a wise Christian man ought to know them and bear them but as the tributes of offending; he ought to bear them manlike and resolvedly, and not as those whining soldiers do, *qui gementes sequuntur imperatorem,* 'who lamenting followed their *imperator.*' (*Ibid.*)

Our Parts in Play of Life.

Seeing God, Who is the author of all our tragedies, hath written out for us and appointed us all the parts we are to play, and hath not, in their distribution, been partial to the most mighty princes of the world; that gave unto Darius the part of the greatest emperor and the part of the most miserable beggar, a beggar begging water of an enemy to quench the great drought of Death; that appointed Bajazet to play the grand signor of the Turks in the morning, and in the same day the footstool of Tamerlane (both which parts Valerian had also played, being taken by Sapores); that made Belisarius play the most victorious captain, and lastly the part of a blind beggar; of which examples many thousands may be produced; why should other men, who are but as the least worms, complain of wrongs? Certainly there is no other account to be made of this ridiculous world, than to resolve that the change of fortune on the great theatre is but as the change of garments on the less; for when, on the one and the other, every man wears but his own skin, the players are all alike. (*Ibid.*)

Death Least *of Evils.*

I have often thought upon Death, and I find it the least of all evils. All that which is past is as a dream, and he that hopes or depends upon time coming dreams waking. So much of our life as we have discovered is already dead; and all those hours which we share even from the breasts of our mothers until we return to our grandmother the Earth, are part of our dying days, whereof even this is one; and those that succeed are of the same nature, for we 'die daily'; and as others have given place to us, so we must in the end give way to others. (*Ibid.*)

Joys of Heaven.

Hereof we are assured that the long and dark night of Death, of whose following day we shall never behold the dawn (till His return that hath triumphed over it), shall cover us over till the world be no more. After which, and when we shall again receive organs glorified and incorruptible, the feats of angelical affections, in so great admiration shall the souls of the blessed be exercised, as they cannot admit the mixture of any second or less joy, nor any return of foregone and mortal affection towards friends, kindred, or children. Of whom, whether we shall retain any particular knowledge, or in any sort distinguish them, no man can assure us, and the wisest men doubt [that is being still on earth]. But, on the contrary, if a divine life retain any of those faculties which the soul exercised in a mortal body, we shall not at that time so divide the joys of Heaven as to cast any part thereof on the memory of their felicities which remain in the world. No; be their estates greater than ever the world gave, we shall (by the difference known unto us) even detest their confideration. And whatfoever comfort shall remain of all forepaft, the fame will confift in the charity which we exercifed living, and in that piety, juftice, and firm faith for which it pleafed the infinite mercy of God to accept of us and receive us. (*Ibid.*)

Frailty of Human Life Unrealized.

Though our own eyes do everywhere behold the fudden and refiftlefs affaults of Death, and Nature affureth us by never-failing experience, and Reafon by infallible demonftration, that our times upon the earth have neither certainty nor durability; that our bodies are but the anvils of pain and difeafes and our minds the hives of unnumbered cares, forrows, and paffions; and that (when we are moft glorified) we are but thofe painted pofts againft which Envy and Fortune direct their darts; yet fuch is the true unhappinefs of our condition and the dark ignorance which covereth the eyes of our underftanding, that we only prize, pamper, and exalt this vaffal and slave of Death [the body], and forget altogether (or only remember at our castaway leisure) the imprisoned immortal soul, which can neither die with the reprobate, nor perish with the mortal parts of virtuous men : seeing God's justice in the one and His greatness in the other is exercised for evermore, on the ever-living subjects of His reward and punishment. But when is it that we examine this great account ? Never while we have one vanity left us to spend: we plead for titles till our breath fail us ; dig for riches while our strength enableth us ; exercise malice while we can revenge ; and then, when time hath beaten from us both youth, pleasure, and health, and that Nature itself hateth the house of Old Age, we remember with Job that 'we must go the way from whence we shall not return,' and 'that our bed is made ready for us in the dark' (x. 21, xvii. 13) ; and then, I say, looking over-late into the bottom of our conscience (which pleasure and ambition had locked up from us all our lives), we behold therein the fearful images of our actions past, and withal the terrible inscription (Eccles. xii. 14) 'that God will bring every work into judgment that man hath done under the sun.' But what examples have ever moved us? what persuasions reformed us? or what threatenings made us afraid? We behold other men's tragedies played before us, we hear what is promised and threatened; but the world's bright glory hath put out the eyes of our minds; and these betraying lights (with which we only see) do neither look up towards termless joys, nor down towards endless sorrows, till we neither know nor can look for anything else at the world's hands. But let us not flatter our immortal souls herein; for to neglect God all our lives and know that we neglect Him, to offend God voluntarily and know that we offend Him, casting our hopes on the peace which we trust to make at parting, is no other than a rebellious presumption, and that which is the worst of all, even a contemptuous laughing to scorn and deriding of God, His laws and precepts: *Frustra sperant qui sic misericordia Dei sibi blandiuntur:* 'They hope in vain,' saith Bernard, 'which in this sort flatter themselves with God's mercy.' (H. W., B. i., c. i.)

'Eloquent' Death.

It is Death that puts into man all the wisdom of the world without speaking a word, which God with all the words of His law, promises or threats, doth not infuse. Death, which hateth and destroyeth man, is believed; God, which hath made him and loves him is always deferred: 'I have considered,' saith Solomon, 'all the works that are under the sun, and behold all is vanity and vexation of spirit' (Eccles. i. 14); but who believes it till Death tells it us? It was Death, which, opening the conscience of Charles the Fifth, made him enjoin his son Philip to restore Navarre; and King Francis the First of France to command that justice should be done upon the murderers of the Protestants in Merindol and Cabrieres, which till then he neglected. It is, therefore, Death alone that can suddenly make man to know himself. He tells the proud and insolent that they are but abjects, and humbles them at the instant, makes them cry, complain, and repent, yea, even to hate their forepast happiness. He takes the account of the rich, and proves him a beggar, a naked beggar, which hath interest in nothing but in gravel that fills his mouth. He holds a glass before the eyes of the most beautiful and makes them see therein their deformity and rottenness, and they acknowledge it.

O eloquent, just, and mighty Death! Whom none could advise thou hast persuaded; what none hath dared thou hast done; and whom all the world hath flattered thou only hast cast out of the world and despised; thou hast drawn together all the far-stretched greatness, all the pride, cruelty, and ambition of men, and covered it all over with these two narrow words—𝔍ic 𝔍acet. (H. W., B. vi., c. vi.)

MORAL GOVERNMENT OF THE UNIVERSE.

Providence.

Providence (which the Greeks call *pronoia*) is an intellectual knowledge, both foreseeing, caring for, and ordering all things, and doth not only behold all

Past, all Present, and all To Come, but is the cause of their so being, which Prescience (simply taken) is not; and therefore Providence, by the philosophers, saith St. Augustine, is divided into memory, knowledge, and care: memory of the Past, knowledge of the Present, and care of the Future; and we ourselves account such a man for provident, as remembering things past, and observing things present, can by judgment, and comparing the one with the other, provide for the future and times succeeding. . . . God, therefore, Who could only be the cause of all, can only provide for all and sustain all; so as to absolute power, to everywhere-presence, to perfect goodness, to pure and divine love (1 John iv. 1), this attribute and transcendent ability of Providence is only proper and belonging. (H. W., B. i., c. i.)

Predestination.

For Predestination, we can difference it no otherwise from Providence and

Prescience, than in this, that Prescience only foreseeth, Providence foreseeth and careth for, and hath respect to all creatures (Rom. viii., ix.), even from the highest angels of heaven to the unworthiest worms of the earth; and predestination (as it is used, especially by divines) is only of men, and yet not of all men belonging, but of their salvation properly, in the common use of divines; or perdition, as some have used it. Yet Peter Lombard (l. i., dist. 39), Thomas (Pt. i., dist. 23), Bernensis Theologus (in Probl., de p. d.), and others, take the word *predestination* more strictly, and for a preparation to felicity. Divers of the Fathers take it more largely sometimes; among whom St. Augustine, speaking of two cities and two societies, useth these words (l. xv., c. i., de Civ. Dei): 'Whereof one is it, which is predestinated to reign for ever with God, but the other is to undergo everlasting torment with the devil'; for according to Nonius Marcellus, *destinare est præparare*. And of the same opinion are many Protestant writers, as Calvin (in c. ix., ad Rom.), Beza (*ibid.*), Buchanus, Danæus, and such like; and as for the manifold questions hereof arising, I leave them to the Divines; and why it hath pleased God to create some vessels of honour and some of dishonour, I will answer with Gregory, who saith, 'He that seeth no reason in the actions of God by consideration of his own infirmity perceiveth the reason of his blindness' (Mag., Job ix.). And again with St. Augustine (ad Polin., ep. 59), 'Hidden the cause of His predestination may be, unjust it cannot be.' (H. W., B. i., c. i.)

Fortune.

Seeing destiny or necessity is subsequent to God's providence, and seeing that the stars have no other dominion than as before spoken, and that Nature is nothing but as Plato called it, 'the art or artificial organ of God,' and Cusanus 'the instrument of the divine precept'; we may with better reason reject that kind of idolatry or god of fools, called Fortune or Chance; a goddess the most reverenced and the most reviled of all other, but not ancient, for Homer maketh her the daughter of Oceanus, as Pausanias witnesseth in his Messeniacks. The Greeks call her τύχην, signifying a relative being or betiding, so as before Homer's time this great lady was scarce heard of; and Hesiod, who hath taught the birth and beginning of all these counterfeit gods, hath not a word of Fortune; yet afterwards she grew so great and omnipotent, as from kings and kingdoms to beggars and cottages she ordered all things, resisting the wisdom of the wisest, by making the possessor thereof miserable; valuing the folly of the most foolish, by making their success prosperous; insomuch as the actions of men were said to be but the sport of Fortune and the variable accidents happening in men's lives but her pastimes. . . . But I will forbear to be curious in that which (as it is commonly understood) is nothing else but a power imaginary, to which the success of human actions and endeavours were for their vanity marked; for when a manifest cause could not be given then was it attributed to Fortune, as if there were no caufe of thofe things of which moft men are ignorant ; contrary to this true ground of Plato, 'Nothing ever came to pafs under the fun of which there was not a juft preceding caufe.' But Aquinas hath herein anfwered in one diftinction, whatfoever may be objected ; for many things there are, faith he, which happen befides the intention of the inferior, but not befides the intention of the fuperior, to wit, the ordinance of God ; and, therefore, faith Melancthon (Sat. x. 366), 'Whom the poets call Fortune we know to be God.' (H. W., B. i., c. i.)

Misfortune and Chance.

It may be objected that if Fortune and Chance were not fometimes the caufes of good and evil in men, but an idle voice whereby we exprefs fuccefs ; how comes it, then, that fo many worthy and wife men depend upon fo many unworthy and empty-headed fools? that riches and honour are given to external men and without kernel, and

Sir Walter Raleigh.

so many learned, virtuous, and valiant men wear out their lives in poor and dejected estates? In a word, there is no other inferior or apparent cause beside the partiality of man's affection, but the fashioning and not fashioning of ourselves according to the nature of the time wherein we live; for whosoever is most able and best sufficient to discern, and hath withal an honest and open heart and loving truth; if princes and those that govern endure no other discourse than their own flatterers, then I say such an one, whose virtue and courage forbiddeth him to be base and a dissembler, shall evermore hang under the wheel, which kind of deserving well and receiving ill we always falsely charge Fortune withal. For whosoever shall tell any great man or magistrate that he is not just, the general of an army that he is not valiant, and great ladies that they are not fair, shall never be made a counsellor, a captain or a courtier. Neither is it sufficient to be wise with a wise prince, valiant with a valiant, and just with him that is just, for such a one hath no estate in his prosperity; but he must also change with the succeffor if he be of contrary qualities; fail with the tide of the time and alter form and condition as the eftate or the eftate's mafter changeth; otherwife how were it poffible that the moft bafe men, and feparate from all imitable qualities, could fo often attain to honour and riches, but by fuch an obfervant, flavifh courfe? Thefe men, having nothing elfe to value themfelves by but a counterfeit kind of wondering at other men, and by making them believe that all their vices are virtues, and all their dufty actions cryftalline, have yet in all ages profpered equally with the moft virtuous, if not exceeded them. For, according to Menander, 'every fool is won with his own pride and others' flattering applaufe,' fo as whofoever will live altogether out of himfelf and ftudy other men's humours, and relieve them, shall never be unfortunate; and, on the contrary, that man which prizeth truth and virtue (except the feafon wherein he liveth be of all thefe and of all forts of goodnefs, fruitful), fhall never profper by the poffeffion or profeffion thereof. It is alfo a token of a worldly-wife man not to war or contend in vain against the nature of times wherein he liveth, for such a one is often the author of his own misery. . . . Whosoever therefore will set before him Machiavel's two marks to shoot at, to wit, riches and glory, must set on and take off a back of iron to a weak wooden bow, that it may fit both the strong and the feeble; for as he that first devised to add sails to rowing vessels did either so proportion them as, being fastened abaft and towards the head of the mast, he might abide all winds and storms, or else he sometime or other perished by his own invention. So that man which prizeth virtue for itself, and cannot endure to hoise and strike his sails as the divers natures of calms and storms require, must cut his sails and his cloth of mean length and breadth, and content himself with a slow and sure navigation, to wit, a mean and free estate. But of this dispute of Fortune and the rest, or of whatsoever lords or gods, imaginary powers or causes, the wit (or rather foolishness) of man hath found out, let us resolve with St. Paul, who hath taught us, that there is 'but one God, the Father, of Whom are all things, and we in Him, and our Lord Jesus Christ, by Whom are all things, and we by Him. There are diversities of operations, but God is the same which maketh all in all' (1 Cor. viii. 6 ; xii. 6). (H. W., B. i., c. i.)

Prescience.

Prescience or Foreknowledge (which the Greeks call *prognosis,* the Latins *præcognitio* or *præscientia*), considered in order and nature (if we may speak of God after the manner of men), goeth before Providence ; for God foreknew all things before He had created them, or before they had being to be cared for ; and Prescience is no other than an infallible foreknowledge. For whatsoever ourselves foreknow, except the same be to succeed accordingly, it cannot be true that we foreknow it. But this prescience of God (as it is prescience only) is not the cause of anything futurely succeeding, neither doth God's foreknowledge impose any necessity or bond. For in that we foreknow that the sun will rise and set; that all men born in the world shall die again; that after winter the spring shall come; after the spring, summer and harvest; and that according to the several seeds that we sow we shall reap several sorts of grain; yet is not our foreknowledge the cause of this, or any of these; neither doth the knowledge in us bind or constrain the sun to rise and set, or men to die; for the causes (as men persuade themselves) are otherwise manifest and known to all (cf. Boethius de Consol.). (H. W., B. i., c. i.)

Accidents so-called.

There is not the smallest accident which may seem unto man as falling out by chance and of no consequence but that the same is caused by God, to effect somewhat else by; yea, and oftentimes to effect things of the greatest worldly importance either presently or in many years after, when the occasions are either not considered or forgotten. (*Ibid.*)

Trifles in Providence.

In Deuteronomy the xixth [verse 5] the flipping of an axe from the helve, whereby another was slain, was the work of God Himself. We in our phrase attribute this accident to chance or fortune. And in Proverbs the xvith: 'The lot is cast into the lap, but the whole disposition thereof is of the Lord' [verse 33]. So as that which seemeth most casual and subject to fortune is yet disposed by the ordinance of God, as all things else. (*Ibid.*)

INJUSTICE OF ARRAIGNMENT OF TREASON, NOV., 1603.

To Lord Cecil of Essingdon.

Sir,—To speak of former times, it were needless. Your Lordship knows what I have been towards yourself, and how long I have loved you and have been favoured by you; but change of times and mine own errors have worn out those remembrances (I fear), and

Sir Walter Raleigh.

if aught did remain yet in the state wherein I stand, there can be no friendship; compassion there may be, for it is never separate from honour and virtue.

If the power of law be not greater than the power of truth, I may justly beseech you to relieve me in this my affliction. If it be, then your Lordship shall have cause (as a just man) to bewail my undeserved miserable estate. I cannot despair but that some warmth remaineth in cinders to move you to the first. To the second I may assure myself that even God Himself and your Lordship's love to justice, will persuade you.

Your Lordship knows my accuser; and have ever known my affection to that nation for which I am accused. A heavy burden of God to be in danger of perishing for a Prince which I have so long hated, and to suffer these miseries under a Prince whom I have so long loved.

Sir, what malice may do against me I know not. My cause hath been handled by strong enemies. But if ever I so much as suspected this practife [= confpiracy] laid to my charge, leave me to death; if the fame by any equity fhall be proved againft me. And *equitas* is faid to be *Juris legitimi emendatio et juſtitiæ directio.*

Your Lordfhip is now a counfellor to a merciful and juft King, if ever we had any. You have ever dealt in matter of juftice, as knowing no man's face; yet vouchfafe now fo to ufe the power which God and the King hath given you, as to defend me from undeferved cruelty. *Potentia non eſt, niſi ad bonum.* The law ought not to overrule piety, but piety the law. The law doth warrant all actions before men, but God hath faid, *Innocentem non interficies.* Your Lordfhip hath known in your time one in this place condemned— and in this place he perifhed—who at the hour of his death received the Sacrament that he was innocent. How, therefore, I fhall be judged I know not. How I have deferved to be judged, I know; and I defire nothing but *fecundum meritum meum.*

If I fhould fay unto the King that my love fo long borne him might hope for fome grace, it would perchance be taken for presumption, because he is a king and my sovereign. But as the King is a true gentleman and a just man, besides his being a king, so he oweth unto me such a merciful respect as the resolution most willingly to have hazarded my life and fortune for him against all men may deserve.

For yourself, my Lord Cecil, and for me, sometime your true friend, and now a miserable forsaken man, I know that affections are neither taught nor persuaded. But if aught remain of good, of love, or of compassion towards me, your Lordship will now show it, when I am most unworthy of your love, and most unable to deserve it. For even then is love, true honour, and true virtue expressed. And what I shall leave to pay [= leave unpaid] of so great a debt, God will perform to your Lordship and to yours. Your Lordship's wretched poor friend and servant,. W. RALEGH.

Your Lordship will find that I have been strangely practised [= conspired] against, and that others have their lives promised to accuse me. I can say no more, but beseech you to use charity:

Charitas eſt quædam participatio Spiritus Sancti. ('Letters,' pp. 278-80.)

BOOKS IN PRISON, 1609.

To Sir Robert Cotton.

SIR ROBERT COTTON,—If you have any of thoſe old books, or any manuſcripts wherein I can read any of our written antiquities, if you pleaſe to lend them me for a little while, I will ſwiftly reſtore them, and think myſelf much beholden unto you ; or if you have any old French hiſtory wherein our nation is mentioned, or any elſe in what language ſoever. — Your poor friend, W. RALEGH. ('Letters,' p. 322 ; Edwards annotates the liſt of long ſince obſolete books, pp. 322, 323. See our Introduction.)

SEIZURE OF SHERBORNE, 1609 (?).

To Sir Robert Carr, after Earl of Somerset.

SIR,—After many great losses and many years' sorrows, of both which I have cause to fear I was mistaken in their ends, it is come to my knowledge that yourself (whom I know not but by an honourable fame), have been persuaded to give me and mine our last fatal blow, by obtaining from his Majesty the inheritance of my children and nephews, lost in law for want of words. This done, there remaineth nothing with me but the bare name of life, despoiled of all else but the title and sorrow thereof. His Majesty, whom I never offended (for I ever held it both unnatural and unmanly to hate goodness), stayed me at the grave's brink; not, as I hope, that his Majesty thought me worthy of many deaths and to behold all mine cast out of the world with myself, but as a king who, judging the poor in truth, hath retained a promise from God that his throne shall be established for ever.

And for yourself, Sir, seeing your day is but now in the dawn and mine come to the evening—your own virtues and the king's grace, assuring you of many good fortunes and much honour — I beseech you not to begin your first buildings upon the ruins of the innocent; and that their griefs and sorrows do not attaint your first plantation. I have been bounden to your nation, as well for many other graces as for the true report of my trial to the king's Majesty, against whom had I been found malignant, the hearing of my cause would not have changed enemies into friends, malice into compassion, and the greatest number present into a commiseration of mine estate. It is not the nature of foul treasons to beget such fair passions; neither would it agree with the duty and love of faithful subjects (especially of your nation) to bewail his overthrow who had conspired against their most blessed and natural Lord. I therefore trust, Sir, that you will not be the first that will kill us outright, cut down the tree with the fruit, and undergo the curse of them that enter into the fields of the fatherless—the which (if it please you to know the truth) are far less fruitful in value than in fame; and that so worthy a gentleman as yourself will rather bind us to your service, being Sir, gentlemen, not base in birth or alliance, who have interest therein. And myself, with the uttermost thankfulness, will ever remain ready to obey your commandments.— W. RALEGH. ('Letters,' pp. 326-328.)

INSTRUCTIONS TO HIS SON AND TO POSTERITY.

§ i. *Virtuous Persons to be made Choice of for Friends.*

There is nothing more becoming any wise man than to make choice of friends; for by them thou shalt be judged what thou art. Let them, therefore, be wise and virtuous, and none of those that follow thee for gain. But make election rather of thy betters than thy inferiors, shunning always such as are poor and needy. For if thou givest twenty gifts and refuse to do the like but once, all that thou hast done will be lost, and such men will become thy mortal enemies. Take also special care that thou never trust any friend or servant with any matter that may endanger thine estate; for so shalt thou make thyself a bondslave to him that thou trustest, and leave thyself always to his mercy. And be sure of this, thou shalt never find a friend in thy young years, whose conditions and qualities will please thee after thou comest to more discretion and judgment; and then all thou givest is lost, and all wherein thou shalt trust such a one will be discovered [= revealed].

Such, therefore, as are thy inferiors will follow thee but to eat thee out, and when thou leavest to feed them they will hate thee; and such kind of men, if thou preserve thy estate, will always be had.

And if thy friends be of better quality than thyself, thou mayest be sure of two things; the first, that they will be more careful to keep thy counsel, because they have more to lose than thou hast; the second, they will esteem thee for thyself, and not for that which thou dost possess.

But if thou be subject to any great vanity or ill (from which I hope God will bless thee), then therein trust no man; for every man's folly ought to be his greatest secret. And although I persuade thee to associate thyself with thy betters, or at least with thy peers, yet remember always that thou venture not thy estate with any of those great ones that shall attempt unlawful things; for such men labour for themselves and not for thee. Thou shalt be sure to part [= share] with them in the danger, but not in the honour; and to venture a sure estate in present, in hope of a better in future, is mere madness.

And great men forget such as have done them service, when they have obtained what they would, and will rather hate thee for saying thou hast been a means of their advancement, than acknowledge it. I could give thee a thousand examples, and I myself know it and have tasted of it in all the course of my life. When thou shalt read and rehearse the stories of all nations, thou shalt find innumerable examples of the like. Let thy love, therefore, be to the best, so long as they do well; but take heed that thou love God, thy country, thy prince, and thine own estate, before all others; for the fancies of men change, and he that loves to-day, hateth to-morrow. But let reason be thy schoolmistress, which shall ever guide thee aright.

§ ii. *Great Care to be had in Choosing of a Wife.*

The next and greatest care ought to be in the choice of a wife; and the only danger therein is beauty, by which all men in all ages, wise and foolish, have been betrayed. And though I know it vain to use reasons or arguments to dissuade thee from being captivated therewith, there being few or none that ever resisted that witchery; yet I cannot omit to warn thee, as of other things, which may be thy ruin and destruction.

For the present time, it is true, that every man prefers his fantasy in that appetite, before all other worldly defires, leaving the care of honour, credit and fafety, in refpect thereof. But remember, that though thefe affections do not laft, yet the bond of marriage dureth to the end of thy life; and therefore better to be borne withal in a miftrefs than as a wife; for when thy humour fhall change thou art yet free to choofe again (if thou give thyfelf that vain liberty). Remember, fecondly, that if thou marry for beauty, thou bindeft thyfelf all thy life for that which, perchance, will never [qu. neither?] laft nor pleafe thee one year; and when thou haft it, it will be to thee of no price at all; for the defire dieth when it is attained, and the affection perifheth when it is fatisfied.

Remember, when thou wert a fucking child, that thou didft love thy nurfe, and thou wert fond of her; after a while thou didft love thy dry-nurfe and didft forget the other; after that thou didft alfo defpife her. So will it be with thy liking in elder years; and therefore, though thou canft not forbear to love, forbear to link; and after a while thou fhalt find an alteration in thyfelf, and see another far more pleasing than the first, second, or third love.

Yet I wish thee above all the rest to have a care thou dost not marry an uncomely woman for any respect; for comeliness in children is riches, if nothing else be left them. And if thou have a care for thy races of horses and other beasts, value the shape and comeliness of thy children, before alliances or riches. Have care, therefore, of both together; for if thou have a fair wife and a poor one, if thine own estate be not great, assure thyself that love abideth not with want; for she is the companion of plenty and honour. For I never yet knew a poor woman exceeding fair that was not made dishonest by one or other in the end. Thus Bathsheba taught her son Solomon: 'Favour is deceitful and beauty is vain.' She wrote further: 'That a wise woman overseeth the ways of her household, and eateth not the bread of idleness' [Proverbs xxxi. 27].

Have, therefore, ever more care that thou be beloved of thy wife, rather than thyself besotted on her; and thou shalt judge of her love by these two observations: first, if thou perceive she has a care of thy estate, and exercise herself therein; the other, if she study to please thee, and be sweet unto thee in conversation, without thy instruction; for love needs no teaching nor precept. On the other side, be not sour or stern to thy wife; for cruelty engendereth no other thing than hatred.

Let her have equal part of thy estate whilst thou livest, if thou find her sparing and honest; but what thou givest after thy death, remember that thou givest it to a stranger, and most times to an enemy: for he that shall marry thy wife will despise thee, thy memory and thine, and shall possess the quiet of thy labours, the fruit which thou hast planted, enjoy thy love, and spend with joy and ease what thou hast spared, and gotten with care and travail.

Yet always remember that thou leave not thy wife to be a shame unto thee after thou art dead, but that she may live according to thy estate; especially if thou hast but few children, and them provided for. But howsoever it be, or whatsoever thou find, leave thy wife no more than of necessity thou must, but only during her widowhood; for if she love again, let her not enjoy her second love in the same bed wherein she loved thee, nor fly to future pleasures with those feathers which Death hath pulled from thy wings ; but leave thy estate to thy house and children, in which thou livest upon earth whilst it lasteth.

To conclude—Wives were ordained to continue the generation of men, not to transfer them and diminish them, either in continuance or ability ; and therefore thy house and estate which liveth in thy son, and not in thy wife, is to be preferred.

Let thy time of marriage be in thy young and strong years ; for believe it, ever the young wife betrayeth the old husband, and she that had thee not in thy flower, will despise thee in thy fall [=Autumn], and thou shalt be unto her but a captivity and sorrow.

Thy best time will be towards thirty ; for as the younger times are unfit, either to choose or to govern a wife and family ; so if thou stay long, thou shalt hardly see the education of thy children, which being left to strangers, are in effect lost ; and better were it to be unborn than ill-bred ; for thereby thy posterity shall either perish or remain a shame to thy name and family. Furthermore, if it be late ere thou take a wife, thou shalt spend thy prime and summer of thy life with harlots, destroy thy health, impoverish thy estate and endanger thy life; and be sure of this, that how many mistresses soever thou hast, so many enemies thou shalt purchase to thyself. For there never was any such affection which ended not in hatred or disdain. Remember the saying of Solomon, 'There is a way which seemeth right to a man, but the issues thereof are the ways of death' [Prov. xiv. 12]; for howsoever a lewd woman please thee for a time, thou wilt hate her in the end and she will study to destroy thee. If thou canst not abstain from them in thy vain and unbridled times, yet remember that thou sowest on the sands and dost mingle thy vital blood with corruption, and purchasest diseases, repentance and hatred only.

Bestow, therefore, thy youth, so that thou mayst have comfort to remember it, when it hath forsaken thee, and not sigh and grieve at the account thereof.

Whilst thou art young thou wilt

think it will never have an end; but behold, the longest day hath his evening; and thou shalt enjoy it but once, for it never [re]turns again.

Use it therefore as the Springtime which soon departeth, and wherein thou oughtest to plant, and sow all provisions for a long and happy life.

§ iii. *Wisest Men have been abused by Flatterers.*

Take care thou be not made a fool by flatterers, for even the wisest men are abused by these.

Know therefore that flatterers are the worst kind of traitors; for they will strengthen thy imperfections, encourage thee in all evils, correct thee in nothing, but so shadow and paint all thy vices and follies, as thou shalt never, by their will, discern evil from good or vice from virtue.

And because all men are apt to flatter themselves, to entertain the additions of other men's praises is most perilous. Do not, therefore, praise thyself except thou wilt be counted a vain-glorious fool; neither take delight in the praise of other men, except thou deserve it, and receive it from such as are worthy and honest, and will withal warn thee of thy faults.

For flatterers have never any virtue. They are ever base, creeping, cowardly persons.

A flatterer is said to be a beast that biteth smiling. It is said by Isaiah in this manner: 'My people, they that praise thee seduce thee and disorder the paths of thy feet' [iii. 12]; and David desired God to cut out the tongue of a flatterer. But it is hard to know them from friends, they are so obsequious and full of protestations.

For as a wolf resembles a dog, so doth a flatterer a friend.

A flatterer is compared to an ape, who, because she cannot defend the house like a dog, labour as an ox, or bear burdens as a horse, doth therefore yet play tricks, and provoke laughter.

Thou mayst be sure that he that will in private tell thee thy faults, is thy friend; for he adventures thy dislike, and doth hazard thy hatred. For there are few men that can endure it, every man for the most part delighting in self-praise, which is one of the most universal follies that bewitcheth mankind.

§ iv. *Private Quarrels to be avoided.*

Be careful to avoid public disputations at feasts, or at tables, among choleric or quarrelsome persons; and eschew evermore to be acquainted or familiar with ruffians; for thou shalt be in as much danger in contending with a brawler in a private quarrel as in a battle, wherein thou mayst get honour to thyself and safety to thy Prince and country; but if thou be once engaged, carry thyself bravely, that they may fear thee after.

To shun, therefore, private fight, be well advised in thy words and behaviour, for honour and shame is in the talk, and the tongue of a man causeth him to fall.

Jest not openly at those that are simple, but remember how much thou art bound to God, who hath made thee wiser.

Defame not any woman publicly,

though thou know her to be evil; for thofe that are faulty cannot endure to be taxed [=accufed or condemned], but will feek to be avenged of thee; and thofe that are not guilty cannot endure unjuft reproach.

And as there is nothing more shameful and difhoneft than to do wrong, fo truth itfelf cutteth his throat that carrieth her publicly in every place.

Remember the divine faying, 'He that keepeth his mouth keepeth his life' [Prov. xiii. 3]. Do, therefore, right to all men where it may profit them, and thou fhalt thereby get much love; and forbear to fpeak evil things of men, though it be true (if thou be not conftrained), and thereby thou fhalt avoid malice and revenge.

Do not accufe any man of any crime, if it be not to fave thyfelf, thy prince, or country; for there is nothing more difhonourable (next to treafon itfelf) than to be an accufer. Notwithftanding, I would not have thee for any refpect lofe thy reputation, or endure public difgrace; for better it were not to live than to live a coward, if the offence proceed not from thyfelf; if it do, it shall be better to compound it upon good terms than to hazard thyself. For if thou overcome thou art under the cruelty of the law, if thou art overcome thou art dead or dishonoured. If thou, therefore, contend, or discourse in argument, let it be with wise and sober men, of whom thou must learn by reasoning, and not with ignorant persons; for thou shalt thereby instruct those that will not thank thee, and will utter what they have learned from thee for their own. But if thou know more than other men, utter it when it may do thee honour, and not in assemblies of ignorant and common persons.

Speaking much, also, is a sign of vanity; for he that is lavish in words is a niggard in deeds; and as Solomon saith: 'The mouth of a wise man is in his heart; the heart of a fool is in his mouth, because what he knoweth or thinketh he uttereth' [xiv. 33].

And by thy words and discourses men will judge thee; for, as Socrates saith, 'Such as thy works are, such will thy affections be esteemed; and such will thy deeds as thy affections, and such thy life as thy deeds.'

Therefore, be advised what thou doſt diſcourſe of, and what thou maintaineſt; whether touching religion, State, or vanity, for if thou err in the firſt thou ſhalt be counted profane; if in the ſecond, dangerous; if in the third, indiſcreet and fooliſh.

He that cannot refrain from much ſpeaking is like a city without walls, and leſs pains in the world a man cannot take than to hold his tongue.

Therefore, if thou obſerveſt this rule in all aſſemblies, thou ſhalt ſeldom err. Reſtrain thy choler, hearken much and ſpeak little; for the tongue is the inſtrument of the greateſt good and greateſt evil that is done in the world. According to Solomon, 'life and death are in the power of the tongue' [xviii. 12]; and as Euripides truly affirmeth, 'Every unbridled tongue in the end ſhall find itſelf unfortunate,' for in all that ever I obſerved in the courſe of worldly things I ever found that men's fortunes are oftener made by their tongues than by their virtues, and more men's fortunes overthrown thereby alſo than by their vices.

And, to conclude, all quarrels, miſchief, hatred, and destruction arise from unadvised speech, and in much speech there are many errors, out of which thy enemies shall ever take the most dangerous advantage. And as thou shalt be happy if thou thyself observe these things, so shall it be most profitable for thee to avoid their companies that err in this kind; and not to hearken to tale-bearers, to inquisitive persons, and such as busy themselves with other men's estates; that creep into houses as spies, to learn news which concerns them not; for assure thyself such persons are most base and unworthy, and I never knew any of them prosper, or respected amongst worthy or wise men.

Take heed, also, that thou be not found a liar; for a lying spirit is hateful both to God and man. A liar is commonly a coward, for he dares not avow truth. A liar is trusted of no man; he can have no credit, either in public or private.

And if there were no more arguments than this, know that our Lord, in St. John, saith, 'that it is a vice proper to Satan' [viii. 44], lying being opposite to the nature of God, which consisteth in truth. And the gain of lying is nothing else but not to be trusted of any, nor to be believed when we say the truth. It is said in the Proverbs that 'God hateth false lips, and he that speaketh lies shall perish' [xix. 9]. Thus thou mayst see and find in all the books of God how odious and contrary to God a liar is; and for the world, believe it, that it never did any man good (except in the extremity of saving life); for a liar is of a base, unworthy, and cowardly spirit.

§ v. *Three Rules to be observed for the Preservation of a Man's Estate.*

Amongst all other things of the world, take care of thy estate, which thou shalt ever preserve, if thou observe three things: first, that thou know what thou hast, what everything is worth that thou hast, and to see that thou art not wasted by thy servants and officers. The second is, that thou never spend anything before thou have it, for borrowing is the canker and death of every man's estate. The third is, that thou suffer not thyself to be wounded for other men's faults, and scourged for other men's offences, which is the surety for another; for thereby millions of men have been beggared and destroyed, paying the reckoning of other men's riot and the charge of other men's folly and prodigality.

If thou smart, smart for thine own sins; and above all things, be not made an ass to carry the burdens of other men.

If any friend desire thee to be his surety, give him a part of what thou hast to spare. If he press thee farther he is not thy friend at all, for friendship rather chooseth harm to itself than offereth it. If thou be bound for a stranger, thou art a fool; if for a merchant, thou puttest thy estate to learn to swim; if for a churchman, he hath no inheritance; if for a lawyer, he will find an evasion by a syllable or word to abuse thee; if for a poor man, thou must pay it thyself; if for a rich man, it need not; therefore from suretyship, as from a manslayer or enchanter, bless thyself, for the best profit and return will be this, that if thou force him for whom thou art bound to pay it himself, he will become thy enemy; if thou use to pay it thyself, thou wilt become a beggar.

And believe thy father in this, and print it in thy thought, that what virtue soever thou haft, be it never so manifold, if thou be poor withal, thou and thy qualities shall be despised. Besides, poverty is oftentimes sent as a curse of God. It is a shame amongst men, an imprisonment of the mind, a vexation of every worthy spirit. Thou shalt neither help thyself nor others; thou shalt drown thee in all thy virtues, having no means to show them; thou shalt be a burden and an eyesore to thy friends, every man will fear thy company, thou shalt be driven basely to beg and depend on others, to flatter unworthy men, to make dishonest shifts; and, to conclude, poverty provokes a man to do infamous and detested deeds. Let not vanity, therefore, or persuasion, draw thee to that worst of worldly miseries.

If thou be rich, it will give thee pleasure in health, comfort in sickness, keep thy mind and body free, save thee from many perils, relieve thee in thy older years, relieve the poor and thy honest friends, and give means to thy posterity to live and defend themselves and thine own fame. Where it is said in the Proverbs that 'he shall be sore vexed that is surety for a stranger, and he that hateth suretyship is sure' [xi. 15], it is further said, 'The poor is hated even of his own neighbour, but the rich have many friends' [xiv. 20]. Lend not to him that is mightier than thyself, for if thou lendest him count it but lost. Be not surety above thy power, for if thou be surety, think to pay it.

§ vi. *What sort of Servants fittest to be Entertained.*

Let thy servants be such as thou mayst command, and entertain none about thee but yeomen, to whom thou givest wages; for those that will serve thee without thy hire will cost thee treble as much as they that know thy fare.

If thou trust any servant with thy purse, be sure thou take his account ere thou sleep; for if thou put it off, thou wilt then afterwards for tediousness neglect it. I myself have, therefore, lost more than I am worth. And whatsoever thy servant gaineth thereby, he will never thank thee, but laugh thy simplicity to scorn; and besides, it is the way to make thy servants thieves, which else would be honest.

§ vii. *Brave Rags wear soonest out of Fashion.*

Exceed not in the humour of rags and bravery, for these will soon be out of fashion; but money in thy purse will ever be in fashion; and no man is esteemed for gay garments, but by fools and women.

§ viii. *Riches not to be sought by Evil Means.*

On the other side, take heed that thou seek not riches basely, nor attain them by evil means; destroy no man for his wealth, nor take anything from the poor, for the cry and complaint thereof will pierce the heavens. And it is moſt deteſtable before God, and moſt diſhonourable before worthy men, to wreſt anything from the needy and labouring foul. God will never proſper thee in aught if thou offend therein.

But uſe thy poor neighbours and tenants well. Give not them and their children to add ſuperfluity and needleſs expenſes to thyſelf. He that hath pity on another man's ſorrow ſhall be free from it himſelf; and he that delighteth in, and ſcorneth the miſery of, another, ſhall one time or another fall into it himſelf. Remember the precept, 'He that hath mercy on the poor lendeth unto the Lord, and the Lord will recompenſe him what he hath given' [xix. 1].

I do not underſtand thoſe for poor which are vagabonds and beggars, but thoſe that labour to live, ſuch as are old and cannot travel, ſuch poor widows and fatherleſs children as are ordered to be relieved, and the poor tenants that travail to pay their rents and are driven to poverty by miſchance, and not by riot or careleſs expenſes. On ſuch have thou compassion, and God will bless thee for it.

Make not the hungry soul sorrowful; defer not thy gift to the needy; for if he curse thee in the bitterness of his soul, his prayer shall be heard of Him that made him.

§ ix. *What inconveniences to such as delight in Wine.*

Take especial care that thou delight not in wine, for there never was any man that came to honour or preferment that loved it. For it transformeth a man into a beast, decayeth health, poisoneth the breath, destroyeth natural heat, brings a man's stomach to an artificial heat, deformeth the face, rotteth the teeth, and, to conclude, maketh a man contemptible, soon old, and despised of all wise and worthy men; hated in thy servants, in thyself, and companions, for it is a bewitching and infectious vice. And remember my words, that it were better for a man to be subject to any vice than to it; for all other vanities and sins are recovered, but a drunkard will never shake off the delights of beastliness. For the longer it possesseth a man the more he will delight in it, and the older he groweth the more he shall be subject to it; for it dulleth the spirits and destroyeth the body as ivy doth the old tree, or as the worm that engendereth in the kernel of the nut.

Take heed, therefore, that such a cureless canker pass not thy youth, nor such a beastly infection thy old age, for then shall all thy life be but as the life of a beast, and after thy death thou shalt only leave a shameful infamy to thy posterity, who shall study to forget that such a one was their father. Anacharsis saith, 'the first draught serveth for health, the second for pleasure, the third for shame, the fourth for madness.' But in youth there is not so much as one draught permitted, for it putteth fire to fire, and wasteth the natural heat and seed of generation. And therefore, except thou desire to hasten thine end, take this for a general rule, that thou never add any artificial heat to thy body, by wine or spice, until thou find that time hath decayed thy natural heat, and the sooner thou beginnest **to** help nature the sooner she will forsake thee and trust altogether **to art.** 'Who have misfortune,' saith Solomon, 'who have sorrow and grief, who have **trouble without** fighting, strifes without **cause,** and faintness of eyes? Even they that sit at wine **and** chain themselves **to empty cups'** [Prov. xxiii. 29]. **Pliny** saith : 'Wine maketh the hand **quivering,** the eyes watery, the night **unquiet,** lewd dreams, **a** stinking breath in the morning, **and** an utter forgetfulness of all things.'

Whosoever loveth wine shall **not be** trusted of any man, for **he** cannot **keep a** secret. Wine maketh man not **only a** beast, but a madman; and if **thou love it,** thy own wife, thy children and thy friends will despise thee. In drink men care **not** what they say, what offence they **give, forget** comeliness, commit disorders, **and, to** conclude, offend all virtuous **and honest** company, and God most **of** all, **to** whom we daily pray **for** health and a **life** free from pain; and yet by drunkenness and gluttonness (which is the drunkenness of feeding) we draw on, saith Hesiod, **'a** swift, hasty, un**timely,** cruel, and an infamous old age.'

And St. Auguſtine deſcribeth drunkenneſs in this manner: 'Drunkenneſs is a flattering devil, a ſweet poiſon, a pleſant ſin, which whoſoever hath hath not himſelf, which whoſoever doth commit doth not commit ſin, but he himſelf is wholly ſin.'

Innocentius ſaith: 'What is filthier than a drunken man, to whom there is ſtink in the mouth, trembling in the body, which uttereth fooliſh things and revealeth ſecret things, whoſe mind is alienate and face transformed? There is no ſecreſy where drunkenneſs rules; nay, what other miſchief doth it not deſign? Whom have not plentiful cups made eloquent and talking?'

When Diogenes ſaw a houſe to be ſold, whereof the owner was given to drink, 'I thought at the laſt,' quoth Diogenes, 'he would ſpue out a whole houſe': *ſciebam inquit, quod domum tandem evomeret.*

§ x. *Let God be thy Protector and Director in all thy actions.*

Now, for the world, I know it too well, to perſuade thee to dive into the practices thereof; rather stand upon thine own guard against all that tempt thee thereunto, or may practise upon thee in thy conscience, thy reputation, or thy purse. Resolve that no man is wise or safe but he that is honest.

Serve God; let Him be the Author of all thy actions; commend all thy endeavours to Him that must either wither or prosper them. Please Him with prayer, lest if He frown He confound all thy fortunes and labours like the drops of rain on the sandy ground.

Let my experienced advice and fatherly instructions sink deep into thy heart. So God direct thee in all His ways, and fill thy heart with His grace. (See our Introduction on this complete Paper.)

'MY OWN TIMES.'

I know that it will be said by many, that I might have been more pleasing to the readers if I had written the story of mine own times, having been permitted to draw water as near the well-head as another. To this I answer, that whosoever in writing a modern history shall follow truth too near the heels, it may happily strike out his teeth. There is no mistress or guide that hath led her followers and servants into greater miseries. He that goes after her too far off, loseth her sight and loseth himself; and he that walks after her at a middle distance, I know not whether I should call that kind of course temper or baseness. It is true that I never travelled after men's opinions when I might have made the best use of them; and I have now too few days remaining to imitate those that, either out of extreme ambition or extreme cowardice, or both, do yet (when Death hath them on his shoulders) flatter the world between the bed and the grave. It is enough for me (being in that state I am) to write of the oldest times; wherein also, why may it not be said, that in speaking of the Past I point at the Present, and tax the vices of those that are yet living in their persons that are long since dead, and have it laid to my charge. But this I cannot help, though innocent. And certainly, if there be any that, finding themselves spotted like the tigers of old time, shall find fault with me for painting them over anew, they shall therein accuse themselves justly, and me falsely. For I protest before the majesty of God, that I malice no man under the sun. Impossible I know it is to please all, seeing few or none are so pleased with themselves, or so assured of themselves, by reason of their subjection to their private passions, but that they seem diverse persons in one and the same day. (Preface, H. W.)

HISTORY—ITS RIGHTS AND DIGNITY.

Among many other benefits for which History hath been honoured, in this one it triumpheth over all human knowledge, that it hath given us life in our understanding, since by it the world itself had life and beginning, even to this day: yea, it hath triumphed over Time, which besides it nothing but Eternity hath triumphed over. For it hath carried our knowledge over the vast and devouring space of so many thousands of years, and given so fair and piercing eyes to our mind, that we plainly behold living now, as if we had lived then, that great world, *magni Dei sapiens opus*—'the wise world,' saith Hermes, 'of a great God'—as it was then, when but new to itself. By it, I say, it is that we live in the very time when it was created; we behold how it was governed; how it was covered with water and again repeopled; how kings and kingdoms have flourished and fallen, and for what virtue and piety God made prosperous, and for what vice and deformity He made wretched, both the one and the other. And it is not the least debt which we owe unto HISTORY, that it hath made us acquainted with our dead ancestors, and out of the depth and darkness of the Earth delivered us their memory and fame. In a word, we may gather out of History a policy no less wise than eternal, by the comparison and application of other men's forepassed miseries with our own like errors and ill-deservings. (*Ibid.*)

ENGLISH v. ROMAN AND FRENCH VALOUR.

Methinks it were not amiss for an Englishman to give such a sentence between the Macedonians and Romans as the Romans once did (being chosen arbitrators) between the Ardeates and Aricini, that strove about a piece of land, saying that it belonged unto neither of them, but unto the Romans themselves. If, therefore, it be demanded whether the Macedonian or the Roman were the best warrior? I will answer 'The Englishman'; for it will soon appear to any that shall examine the noble acts of our Nation in war, that they were performed by no advantage of weapon, against no savage or unmanly people; the enemy being far superior unto us in numbers and all needful provisions, yea, as well trained as we, or commonly better, in the exercise of war.

In what sort Philip won his dominions in Greece; what manner of men the Persians and Indians were, whom Alexander vanquished; as likewise of what force the Macedonian phalanx was, and how well appointed againſt ſuch arms as it commonly encountered, any man that hath taken pains to read the ſtory of them doth ſufficiently underſtand. Yet was this phalanx never, or very ſeldom, able to ſtand againſt the Roman armies, which were embattled in ſo excellent a form as I know not whether any nation beſides them have uſed, either before or ſince. The Roman weapons likewiſe, both offenſive and defenſive, were of greater uſe than thoſe with which any other nation hath ſerved, before the fiery inſtruments of gunpowder were known. As for the enemies with which Rome had to do, we find that they which did overmatch her in numbers were as far overmatched by her in weapons, and that they of whom ſhe had little advantage in arms had as little advantage of her in multitude. This alſo (as Plutarch well obſerveth) was a part of her happineſs, that ſhe was never overlaid with two great wars at once.

It is not my purpoſe to diſgrace the Roman valour, which was very noble, or to blemiſh the reputation of ſo many famous victories; I am not so idle. This I say, that among all their wars I find not any wherein their valour hath appeared comparable to the English. If my judgment seem over-partial, our wars in France may help to make it good.

First, therefore, it is well known that Rome, or perhaps all the world besides, had never any so brave a commander in war as Julius Cæsar, and that no Roman army was comparable unto that which served under the same Cæsar. Whence it is apparent that this gallant army, which had given fair proof of the Roman courage in good performance of the Helvetian War, when it entered into Gaul, was nevertheless utterly disheartened when Cæsar led it against the Germans. So that we may justly impute all that was extraordinary in the valour of Cæsar's men to their long exercise under so good a leader in so great a war. Now let us in general compare with the deeds done by those best of Roman soldiers in their principal service, the things performed in the same country by our common English soldier, levied in haste from following the cart or fitting on the shop-stall; so we shall see the difference. Herein will we deal fairly, and believe Cæsar in relating the acts of the Romans; but will call the French historians to witness what actions were performed by the English. (H. W.)

TO HIS MISTRESS, QUEEN ELIZABETH.

Wrong not, sweet empress of my heart,
    The merit of true passion,
With thinking that he feels no smart
    That sues for no compassion.

Since, if my plaints serve not t' approve
    The conquest of thy beauty,
It comes not from defect of love,
    But from excess of duty.

For, knowing that I sue to serve
    A saint of such perfection,
As all desire, but none deserve,
    A place in her affection.

Sir *Walter Raleigh.*

I rather choose to want relief
    Than venture the revealing:
Where glory recommends the grief,
    Despair distrusts the healing.

Thus those desires that aim too high
    For any mortal lover,
When Reason cannot make them die,
    Discretion doth them cover.

Yet, when discretion doth bereave
    The plaints that they should utter,
Then thy discretion may perceive
    That silence is a suitor.

Silence in love bewrays more woe
    Than words, though ne'er so witty:
A beggar that is dumb, you know,
    May challenge double pity.

Then wrong not, dearest to my heart,
    My true, though secret, passion;
He smarteth most that hides his smart,
    And sues for no compassion.

A POESY TO PROVE AFFECTION IS NOT LOVE.

[*Before* 1602.]

Conceit, begotten by the eyes,
Is quickly born and quickly dies;
For while it seeks our hearts to brave,
Meanwhile there Reason makes his grave;
For many things the eyes approve,
Which yet the heart doth seldom move.

For as the seeds in Spring-time sown
Die in the ground ere they be grown,
Such is conceit, whose rooting fails
As child that in the cradle quails,
Or else within the mother's womb
Hath his beginning and his tomb.

Affection follows Fortune's wheels,
And soon is shaken from her heels;
For following beauty or estate,
Her liking still is turned to hate;
For all affections have their change,
And Fancy only loves to range.

Desire himself runs out of breath,
And, getting, doth but gain his death;

Sir Walter Raleigh.

Desire nor reason hath not rest,
And, blind, doth seldom choose the best;
Desire attained is not desire,
But as the cinders of the fire.

As ships in port desired are drowned,
As fruit, once ripe, then falls to ground,
As flies that seek for flames are brought
To cinders by the flames they sought;
So fond desire, when it attains,
The life expires, the woe remains.

And yet some poets fain would prove
Affection to be perfect love,
And that desire is of that kind
No less a passion of the mind;
As if wild beasts and men did seek
To like, to love, to choose alike.

VERSES FOUND IN HIS BIBLE IN THE GATEHOUSE AT WESTMINSTER, 1618.

[*Transcribed by Sancroft, Archbishop of Canterbury.*]

Even such is time, that takes in trust
   Our youth, our joy, our all we have,
And pays us but with earth and dust;
   Who, in the dark and silent grave,
When we have wander'd all our ways,
Shuts up the story of our days;
But from this earth, this grave, this dust,
My God shall raise me up, I trust.

THE END.

Elliot Stock, 62, *Paternoster Row*, London, E.C.

www.ingramcontent.com/pod-product-compliance
Lightning Source LLC
Chambersburg PA
CBHW020823230426
43666CB00007B/1076